The Corrosion of Charity
From Moral Renewal to Contract Culture

For

MAX GAMMON

in recognition of his leadership in
the campaign for the restoration of Barts
to independent charitable status.

The IEA Health and Welfare Unit

Choice in Welfare No. 29

The Corrosion of Charity

From Moral Renewal to Contract Culture

Robert Whelan

IEA Health and Welfare Unit
London, 1996

First published July 1996

The IEA Health and Welfare Unit
2 Lord North St
London SW1P 3LB

© The IEA Health and Welfare Unit 1996

ISBN 0-255 36367-2

Cover artwork from CorelDraw 6

Typeset by the IEA Health and Welfare Unit
in New Century Schoolbook 10 on 11 point
Printed in Great Britain by
St Edmundsbury Press
Blenheim Industrial Park, Newmarket Road
Bury St Edmunds, Suffolk IP33 3TU

Contents

Foreword

For much of this century the state has progressively widened its embrace of welfare provision, so that today many find it hard to imagine any alternative. In *The Corrosion of Charity* Robert Whelan shows how some of the famous charities of the nineteenth century often did a better job than the welfare state that displaced them. Because of their focus on individual reformation, they never gave up on anyone, insisting that all were capable of self-improvement. Today, surviving charities have often been so thoroughly permeated by the assumptions of the statutory agencies that their formal independence is of little significance. Far from having boundless confidence in the potential of every individual to change, they are more likely to denounce any focus on the individual as scape-goating or 'blaming the victim' and to demand instead, the structural reform of society. This corrosion of the true charitable spirit has been the result of growing reliance on government grants.

Robert Whelan's study forms part of a long-standing project initiated by Arthur Seldon intended to revitalise our understanding of how health, education and welfare were provided before the welfare state. Professor E.G. West's *Education and the State* (1965) was the first study, revealing the extent of private schooling before the 1870 Forster Act. After a long gap, attention was turned to medical care before the welfare state in *The Welfare State: For Rich or For Poor* (1982) and *Working Class Patients and the Medical Establishment* (1984). Later still, *Reinventing Civil Society* (1993) looked at private social security, and showed how the friendly societies were already providing for more than three-quarters of those covered by the 1911 National Insurance Act.

Robert Whelan's study of charitable endeavour helps to fill in another piece of the jigsaw. Its particular strength is his discussion of the decisive role played by Christian churches in upholding a tradition of self-sacrificing service of the poor.

David G. Green

The Author

Robert Whelan is the Assistant Director of the Health and Welfare Unit of the Institute of Economic Affairs. He has written and produced a series of videos on social and medical issues including *The Truth about AIDS, Facing Facts on Population* and *The Three R's of Family Life*. His publications include *Mounting Greenery,* IEA Education Unit 1988; *Choices in Childbearing*, Committee on Population and the Economy 1992; *Broken Homes and Battered Children* and *Teaching Sex in Schools*, Family Education Trust 1994 and 1995; and (with Roger Cummins) *Making a Lottery of Good Causes*, IEA Health and Welfare Unit, 1995.

Acknowledgements

I must, first of all, acknowledge my indebtedness to Alejandro Chafuen, President of the Atlas Economic Research Foundation in Fairfax, Virginia, his directors and staff. Without the financial support and personal kindness which they extended to me as an Atlas Research Fellow in the summer of 1995 this book could not have been written.

I am also indebted for advice and assistance to many people, chief amongst whom are Patrick Carroll; Roger Singleton and Michael Jarman of Barnardos; Major Jenty Fairbank, Major Ray Oakley and Gordon Taylor of the Salvation Army; David Green of the IEA Health and Welfare Unit; Frank Prochaska; Jim Richards of the Catholic Children's Society (Westminster); Rev Stephen Roberts of Trinity in Camberwell; Ian Sparks, David Lovell and Ian Wakeling of The Children's Society; Rachel Tingle of the Christian Studies Centre; Peter Watherston of the Mayflower Family Centre; and Tom White of NCH Action for Children. Needless to say, none of the above are responsible for the book's conclusions, which are wholly my own. I would also like to thank those who generously participate in the IEA's blind refereeing process, which resulted in many helpful comments on the text.

Introduction

THE realisation that something has gone badly wrong with welfare is now accepted by almost all shades of the political spectrum, and the reform of the welfare state is being seriously canvassed. However, many of those who are fully aware of its defects still feel obliged to defend the welfare state out of fear of what would happen if it were to be circumscribed. State welfare, with all of its manifest inefficiencies and perverse incentives, is felt to be preferable to leaving the poor to starve on the streets.

This is to assume that the alternative to state welfare is no welfare. It has been part of the mission of the Health and Welfare Unit of the IEA to carry out and publicise research into methods by which welfare provision was made before the intrusion of the state into this field. David Green's research into the friendly societies for mutual aid which flourished in the last century is well-known.[1] These enormously popular institutions enabled working people, including the low paid, to make their own provisions for medical treatment, sickness and other benefits.

But what happened to those who could not provide for their needs in this way, either because they were too poor to keep up even the low level of payments required, or because they were in irregular employment?

For hundreds of years the state had accepted the ultimate responsibility for the relief of poverty through the poor law, with the uninviting prospect of the workhouse to discourage what the Elizabethans called 'lustie beggars', and what we would call welfare scroungers. However, there was another, far more important source of relief coming not from the state, but from charity.

It is difficult for those who have grown up under a welfare state to grasp the nature and extent of the charitable sector before the state assumed the role of welfare provider-in-chief. England has the richest tradition of philanthropy in the world, which reached its peak in the last part of the nineteenth century. The vast network of charitable societies which had been formed to supply every imaginable need represented a sort of private-sector welfare state.

The majority of these charities were the expression of religious faith, although for some philanthropists the simple humanitarian urge to relieve suffering would have provided a sufficient motive, with or without a fervent spiritual imperative. One thing which united the philanthropists, whatever their motives, was the belief that people in need should be helped in ways which did not undermine their dignity and self-respect. In particular, it was felt that people who, for whatever reason, were dependent on outside assistance should be enabled to regain their independence as soon as possible, unless they were physically or mentally incapacitated from doing so. Charity was intended to help people over a bad patch and to restore them to full participation in society, offering support for them in their weaknesses in a way which would develop their strengths.

This study examines the ways in which the British people have responded to the biblical command to feed the hungry, clothe the naked and tend the sick (Mt.25:34-46). It also asks what lessons we can learn from the past as we contemplate alternatives to the welfare state. The contemporary prejudice against charity ('cold as') should not blind us to the possibility that the private provision of welfare may have had strengths which we have neglected to our cost. With the government now spending more than its entire revenue from income tax on a welfare system which seems to actually increase the very problems it is supposed to be addressing, it is at least worth asking if anyone has ever had a better idea.

Early Charitable Traditions

RICHARD Titmuss once wrote that, when we study welfare systems, we see that they reflect the dominant cultural and political characteristics of their societies. The Church provided welfare services for the Catholic middle ages; the wealthy merchants of Tudor and Stuart England took on the responsibility from the Church; and the period following the Restoration of the monarchy in 1660 took from the economic life of the country the principle which was to become the pattern for charitable work down to our own day: the joint stock venture.

The Reformation of charity

The Protestant Reformation which swept northern Europe in the sixteenth century brought the monastic provision of welfare services to a close. The Catholic Church was 'dis-established' in one country after another, its assets confiscated, its churches and religious houses closed, and its activities in welfare provision brought to an end. The immediate cause of the Reformation in England was the desire of King Henry VIII to annul his marriage with Katherine of Aragon in order to marry Ann Boleyn, and the refusal of Pope Clement VII to grant the necessary dispensation. However, given the triumph of the ideas of Calvin and Luther in Germany, the Netherlands, Switzerland and Scandinavia, it seems likely that Protestantism would have reached English shores with or without Ann Boleyn's assistance.

It is not within the scope of this book to consider the causes or consequences of the Protestant Reformation, except in so far as they affect the provision of welfare services. This effect, in England, was that the poor were left largely unprovided for, although it has to be said that the monastic foundations had been in decline for some time prior to the Reformation, so it was not exactly a case of going from a flourishing medieval church welfare operation to nothing overnight. Henry VIII promised to replace the monastic hospitals with other foundations, paid for by the government, but this promise remained unfulfilled. Only three of the medieval hospitals (which were as much for the care of the poor and the elderly as the sick) survived the Reformation to be re-constituted as secular foundations, all of them in London: St Bartholomew's, St Thomas' and Bethlehem (Bedlam). There was no further hospital building in London until the eighteenth century. The confiscated assets of the religious houses went to pay for other areas of government expenditure or to enrich the nobility. For several decades the poor were left to fend for themselves.

A Secular Society

The classic study of welfare and charity for this period is W.K. Jordan's *Philanthropy in England: 1480—1660*.[1] The basis of Jordan's book was his examination of all charitable gifts recorded in ten counties of England between 1480 and 1660. His counties contained about a third of the population and about a half of the wealth in the country (as London was included). Most of the benefactions which Jordan was able to trace were included in wills, and he worked on the assumption that the way in which men dispose of their worldly goods when they are on the verge of meeting their maker is a reasonable indication of their priorities.

His study covered the period bridging the decline of medieval society and the emergence of the modern world. It was much more than a transition from Catholic to Protestant: in Jordan's view the growth of capitalism and the overthrow of a social system in which the universal church had played an enormously important part represented nothing less than a transition from an intensely religious society to a profoundly secular one. The attack on ignorance and superstition, which were regarded by reformers as characteristics of the Catholic church, signified a determination to get to grips with the problems of this life and an unwillingness to dwell for very long on the mysteries of the life to come.

This fundamental shift in attitudes had a profound effect on charitable giving. Using the evidence he had collected from wills and other sources, Jordan showed how the traditional medieval bequests to abbeys and churches, often accompanied by mass offerings for the repose of the soul of the donor, were replaced by other, more secular concerns, such as the relief of poverty. But even the attitude towards poverty had changed. Instead of being regarded as an unavoidable misfortune, like bad weather, poverty was viewed increasingly as a preventable problem, susceptible to scientific analysis, and often stemming from personal habits which could be changed. The typical form of medieval assistance to the poor, according to Jordan, was the 'dole', the gift of money, food or other benefits made at the monastery gates or at the funeral of some great man. No attempt was made to distinguish between the worthy and unworthy recipients of the dole by inquiring into the causes of their poverty, or the degree of real need. They were poor—or presented themselves as poor—and the biblical injunction was to relieve poverty. That was the end of the analysis.

Such alms-giving had the potential for causing social problems. The structural changes in the economy of the late middle ages, particularly in agriculture, had already resulted in large numbers of men becoming unemployed as arable land was turned over to pasture. Wandering about the country looking for work, many of these men became beggars and vagabonds. The distribution of lavish doles attracted swarms of these vagrants and presented a serious threat to law and order, with drunken celebrations continuing for days. More seriously, by giving out doles without making any inquiry into the circumstances of the recipients, it perpetuated what we would call welfare dependency and what in the sixteenth century were referred to as 'lustie beggars'—people who were quite capable of working but saw no need to.

Jordan took the view that the citizens of Tudor England were forced to cope with such great forces of social and economic dislocation that the old view of poverty simply would not serve. There was, in fact, a new sort of poverty which, if not dealt with, could have caused the social fabric to unravel:

> ... after the beginning of the fourteenth century ... various ecclesiastical institutions, and most particularly the monasteries and the many hospitals, began to assume a larger role in the relief of at least conspicuous indigence, while in the towns the craft guilds in their various forms undertook, usually under ecclesiastical auspices, the most effective social insurance and concern that the medieval world was to know. Then came the immense disaster accompanying the decline of the mediæval society, resulting in a steady decay of institutions and of social attitudes, a process not yet complete as our period began. The decay of manors, the savage and destructive waves of plague, foreign and internecine wars, and the slow erosion of civil and economic order not only vastly worsened the problem of poverty but spawned a new kind of poor with which the sixteenth century sought to deal in an amazed and awkward incertitude.[2]

Poor Laws and Charitable Trusts

Jordan argued that the response to this dangerously unstable situation was two-pronged. It involved, on the one hand, the passage of the Poor Laws, and on the other the clarification of the laws governing charitable trusts.

The passage of the great Act for the Relief of the Poor in 1597 codified earlier provisions to set up a system of relief which would prevent the spectacle of death from starvation on the streets, and would hopefully tackle the serious problem of beggars and vagrants. As Catholic critics were later to suggest, the Poor Law was inspired, at least in part, by the need to put something in place of the system of poor relief which had been swept away with the monasteries. The authorities were only too well aware that unfavourable comparisons with the old system could have proved an incendiary factor to ignite what was still a very widespread resentment at Henry VIII's confiscation of church property. Furthermore, the severe economic depression of the 1590s, made worse by a series of wet summers and bad harvests, and compounded by the war with Spain, had combined to make large-scale civil unrest a real possibility.

The Poor Law of 1597 therefore established overseers in every parish with the authority to raise a local rate which would be used to set to work the poor and unemployed, and to apprentice their children. The overseers were also to provide sustenance for 'the lame, impotent, old, blind and such other among them being poor and not able to work'. Such relief would only be made available to the poor in the parish of their birth. This was intended to prevent vagrancy by 'sealing up' the problem of poverty on a local basis.

The overseers of the Poor Law in each parish were to be the church wardens and 'four other substantial householders'. No clergyman was mentioned in the Act, and although the parish was used as the administrative unit, the church was to have no role to play in the administration of the Poor Law at all. This was of great significance because it marked a critical stage in the transition from the view that the church should take care of the poor to the modern view that poverty is a problem to be handled by the institutions of secular society.

The aim of the Poor Law was to support those who could not be helped in any other way. It embodied the distinction which had been an essential part of poor law provision since a statute of 1531 that the worthy and unworthy poor had to be separated, with the unworthy—professional beggars and rogues—confined to houses of correction, and vagabonds whipped back to their own parishes. The Poor Law was a safety net, intended to be brought into play in emergencies, and discontinued as soon as circumstances allowed.

For the most part, however, the problem of poverty was regarded as being within the remit of private and charitable action, and it is in this connection that the passage of the statute of charitable trusts in 1597 (the same year as the Poor Law) was important. Like the Poor Law, the statute did not set up anything new in English law: there had been trusts as far back as the thirteenth century, and the endowment of trusts had become increasingly common since about 1520. However the 1597 statute was, in Jordan's phrase, a great 'gathering act':[3] it gave classical expression to a rather disorganised corpus of laws, and thus gave potential benefactors the assurance that whatever they bequeathed to good works under deed of trust would continue to be used for that purpose in perpetuity.

The intention of the Trust Law was to open the floodgates of private charity to solve social problems, with the Poor Law provisions held in reserve for cases of emergency such as failed harvests, wars and the plague. As Jordan demonstrates with many pages of statistics, the attempt to persuade private citizens to assume civic responsibility was successful:

> The immediate, and perhaps the expected, consequence of the passage of this great *corpus* of legislation was a notable increase in the flow of private charitable funds designed to provide relief for the truly derelict and to attack the whole problem of poverty frontally by creating institutions which would effect its cure. ... in the one generation following the passage of the Elizabethan poor laws rather more was given for charitable uses than in the whole of the preceding four.[4]

Moreover, he was able to show that the Poor Law was only rarely invoked, and in some areas never invoked at all up until 1660. The extent to which public funds, raised by the imposition of a rate, contributed towards the relief of poverty was, in Jordan's view, negligible:

... at no time in our period were the sums raised by rates substantial or particularly significant when compared with the great amounts available as a consequence of the ever-mounting endowments created by private generosity ... the most liberal analysis of the data ... would seem to suggest that in no year prior to 1660 was more than 7 per cent of all the vast sums expended on the care of the poor derived from taxation. We believe that this is not far from the mark for England as a whole, in great areas of which rates for poor relief were never levied at all ... The great corpus of Elizabethan law was, as we have seen, a prudential system, framed to protect the society and the state against the threat of social disaster which might have become very real indeed had not private men acted so quickly, so generously, and so intelligently as they addressed themselves to the mastery of the transcendent problems of their age.[5]

Deflating the Figures

Jordan's analysis has been challenged by subsequent historians. It has been pointed out that he failed to take into account either the growth of population or, more seriously, the severe inflation which eroded the value of the benefactions he catalogues.[6] However J.F. Hadwin reviewed the objections to Jordan's work in an article for *Economic History Review* and came to the conclusion that, although Jordan had overstated his case, his main points still held true after allowing for population growth and inflation. There was indeed a growth in charitable giving over the period, particularly for the relief of poverty, with a fourfold expansion in poor relief at a time when the population cannot have increased more than twofold.

Charitable Purposes

Whatever the truth about the relative levels of giving over the period, Jordan's main point seems to be beyond dispute. There was a fundamental change in the way in which poverty and its relief came to be regarded.

Jordan's thesis was that the wealthy merchants and gentry of his period had a more long-term view of relieving poverty than their forebears. For them, cash donations or 'doles' were not a sufficient response: the important thing was to eliminate poverty permanently by making the poor self-supporting. Of all the different branches of philanthropy which he examines, none demonstrates this more clearly than education. Founding schools, and in particular grammar schools for the education of poor scholars, was a sort of obsession of the age. Donations for education accounted for over a quarter of all charitable giving in the period, and resulted in a total of 437 schools being founded and endowed by the residents of the ten counties in Jordan's study, many of which are still extant today. A large proportion of these were grammar schools, and almost all provided free education for poor boys. This was seen as the real way to tackle poverty. By equipping bright young people with a proper education, they would be enabled to participate in the burgeoning capitalist economy, not only supporting themselves and their families but making a vital contribution to the dramatic economic transformation which was taking place in England at the time. As Jordan put it:

> With £403 5s 4d [the average worth of all the trusts established over the period] a late fifteenth century landed magnate could arrange funeral doles which were certain to attract unruly swarms of beggars from a half dozen nearby counties; with the same amount a Norwich merchant a century later could endow in perpetuity a social institution of great and abiding utility.[7]

Puritans vs. 'Fat Bellyed Monkes'

Jordan illustrated the secular drift of charitable activity by citing the famous preamble to the 1597 Act on charitable trusts which stated that wealth had been left by sovereigns and:

> ... by sondrie other well disposed persons, some for releife of aged impotent and poore people, some for maintenance of sicke and maymed souldiers and marriners, schooles of learninge, free schooles and schollers in universities, some for repaire of bridges portes havens causewaies churches seabankes and highwaies, some for education and preferments of orphans, some for or towardes reliefe stocke or maintenance for howses of correction, some for marriages of poore maides, some for supportacion ayde and helpe of younge tradesmen, handie-craftesmen and persons decayed, and others for releife or redemption of prisoners or captives, and for aide or ease of any poore inhabitants concerning paymente of fifteenes, [and] settinge out of souldiers and other taxes.

His comment on this is significant:

> The conception and definition of charitable purposes here advanced was starkly and coldly secular, just as were the benefactions of the age. The only religious purpose mentioned at all was the repair of churches, and even this was quite inconspicuously tucked in between 'causewaies' and 'seabankes'. This omission was flagrantly deliberate, because the whole temper of the age had grown so completely secular and because the preoccupations of men had fastened so tenaciously on the many and pressing needs of the world and the society which they saw about them. In point of fact, even the repair of a parish church, very rarely undertaken in Elizabethan England, was itself a quasi-civic undertaking, the motives for which were quite as likely to proceed from local pride as from religious sentiment.[8]

Jordan's view that charitable bequests reveal an increasingly secular society was challenged by Eamon Duffy in his book *The Stripping of the Altars*. Duffy argued that the cessation of gifts to guilds and bequests to pay for masses to be said for the soul of the deceased represented nothing more than a rational reaction to political events. The religious guilds had been dissolved in 1547, and the belief in purgatory and masses for the dead was being denounced by church and state. Any will containing such provisions would probably have been overturned in the ecclesiastical courts.[9]

However, there was nothing to stop people from building or enriching churches and cathedrals: the fact is that they hardly ever did so. There was virtually no new church building at all in England for two hundred years after the Reformation, and the churches which survived the attention of the Reformers were allowed to decay in a way which many regarded as scandalous. The Protestants, and particularly the Puritans, were generous in supporting good causes: they just did not seem to regard building or beautifying churches as a good cause. The only major church building project to be undertaken during the period was the massive rebuilding of St Paul's Cathedral at the beginning of the seventeenth century. This was promoted by Archbishop Laud and involved the extraction of large donations from the merchant princes of the City of London, many of whom were Puritans and consequently bitterly resentful of being pressured into supporting a religious work which was offensive to them.

However, to say that the thrust of Tudor and Stuart philanthropy was secular is not to say that the benefactors were irreligious men. Quite the contrary, in fact, as the enormous surge in giving which characterised the first four decades of the seventeenth century co-incided with the rise of Puritanism and Calvinism. These men was just as concerned with questions of heaven and hell as their Catholic forebears, and saw charitable giving as an important expression of their faith. However, in the area of good works, they expressed their concerns in a very different way from their ancestors.

The Philanthropy of the Common Man

The next major development in the field of philanthropy was the application of the principle of the joint stock company to charitable works. This principle was the very simple one of pooled resources. Instead of looking to a small number of wealthy individuals for capital, companies were formed which took small amounts of capital from large numbers of not-so-wealthy supporters, or shareholders. The joint stock boom of the 1690s threw up hundreds of examples of such companies, honest and dishonest, prosperous and bankrupt.

The application of the same principle to charitable undertakings seems obvious to us now, but it was revolutionary in its day. In previous ages, charitable works like the foundation of schools and almshouses had represented the benefaction of a wealthy man, often on his deathbed. The principle of associated philanthropy (as it has come to be known) meant that large numbers of the living could pool what might be, in individual cases, very limited resources to achieve similarly impressive goals.

The first large-scale application of the new approach came with the foundation of the Society for Promoting Christian Knowledge (SPCK) by Rev Thomas Bray in 1699. The original aim was to create a Protestant alternative to the Roman Catholics' Congregation for the Doctrine of the Faith, but this proved to be over-ambitious. Dr Bray and his associates contented themselves with a rather vague commitment to 'promote Christian knowledge' as an antidote to the vice and immorality of the age. However, what really put the SPCK into the annals of charity history was its involvement with charity schools.

Charity schools—that is to say, schools for the poor not teaching a classical curriculum—were not entirely new, nor did SPCK run schools itself. It acted as a sort of clearing house of ideas, encouraging vicars and congregations up and down the country to start schools, providing advice, contacts and suggestions for the curriculum. In the words of the historian of the charity schools, the SPCK was able to weld together 'the separate and occasional charity of the benevolent into an organised movement for the education of the poor'.[10]

The movement enjoyed great success almost from the start. Five years after its launch there were 54 schools in London alone, and by 1729 there were 1,419 schools in England educating 22,503 children. Some schools benefited from endowments, while others survived on a more precarious basis of subscriptions—i.e. the constant solicitation of funds from supporters. By the middle of the eighteenth century the movement had peaked, and the SPCK began to turn its attention elsewhere as a result of factional divisions which had arisen over the control of the schools. In spite of the problems, some of the schools survive today, and although the charity school movement itself went into decline, it had established amongst Christians the idea that voluntary associations for the education of the poor were praiseworthy. The principle was to re-emerge later in the Sunday School and Ragged School movement.

David Owen, in his history of English philanthropy, sums up the importance of the charity school movement:

> Despite its manifest shortcomings, this first large-scale venture in associated philanthropy offered a convincing demonstration of what could be accomplished by the pooling of individual effort. Not only that but, more specifically, the pattern of a central committee guiding the work of numbers of local committees became a commonplace in organising good works on a national scale. In dozens of other causes the same technique was employed, and, in some degree, the charity school movement supplied the model which was unconsciously followed by subsequent reforming and philanthropic enterprises.[11]

The Care of the Sick

As the charity schools movement was reaching its zenith, another exercise on the principle of associated philanthropy was getting under way which was to have even more profound and lasting social consequences.

By the early eighteenth century it had become obvious that the three hospitals in London which had survived the Reformation—St Bartholomew's, St Thomas' and Bethlehem (Bedlam)—were pitifully inadequate to meet the healthcare needs of one of the world's greatest cities. Furthermore, the perceived role of hospitals had changed. In medieval times hospitals were places for the care of the sick, the poor, the elderly, the disabled, travellers and others. Given the very limited state of medical knowledge at the time there was, in any case, very little which could be done for the sick beyond preparing them for the next life.

Advances in medical science, coupled with the immense population growth of London, created the demand for more hospitals which would not only offer more specialised treatment but which would also provide teaching facilities for doctors. Within less than three decades no fewer than five of the great London teaching hospitals were founded, all of which still exist (just) today: the Westminster (1720), Guy's (1725) St George's (1733), the London (1740) and the Middlesex (1745). Guy's was the result of the munificence of Thomas Guy, a wealthy businessman whose chief pleasure in life was philanthropy. He made a killing in the City by selling his South Sea shares for nearly £235,000, just before the bubble burst, and found himself in a position to build a new hospital. He did not survive to see the completion of his plan, but Guy's was made the residuary legatee on his estate and found itself with an endowment of over £220,000.[12]

However, Guy's was an exceptional establishment which could hardly have set a trend. The other four hospitals were built on the principle of associated philanthropy, and, by means of the vast sums which they were able to attract in donations from the public, established medical charities in the pre-eminent position which they still enjoy in the public's favour.[13] These London hospitals, together with others which were established in the provinces, laid the foundations of the voluntary hospital movement which was to become one of the great achievements of English philanthropy. The voluntary hospitals were secular foundations, and indeed Britain is unusual amongst European nations in having no significant tradition of Christian hospitals, but the motivation of their founders and supporters had, in many cases, been religious. According to David Owen:

> Ordinary humanitarianism was probably the main impulse actuating those ... who promoted the hospital movement. But humanitarians, certainly English humanitarians, more often than not were men of sincere and sometimes fervent religious beliefs. For them charity was a Christian duty, and in providing medical care for the poor they were carrying out the Divine injunction.[14]

The Foundling Hospital

The new hospitals undoubtedly represented the most important new development in eighteenth century philanthropy, as they established the voluntary hospital movement. This was to grow into a system for the delivery of health care which was extensive, efficient and unique to Britain. However if we are looking for a philanthropic venture which encapsulated the spirit of the age of reason and the enlightenment, we would have to settle on Captain Coram's Foundling Hospital.

By the beginning of the eighteenth century Britain was almost alone amongst European nations in having no provision for orphaned or abandoned children. Thomas Coram, a retired sea captain living in

Rotherhithe, became so distressed by the sight of infants left to die in the street that he resolved to establish a hospital, or orphanage, for their care. He felt that the absence of any such provision was an offence to the conscience of a Christian nation, and a disgrace to a great capital city.

However, he soon found that he had embarked on an undertaking of the greatest complexity. In order to accept responsibility for the upbringing of children, and to solicit donations and bequests from the public, he needed a Royal Charter. His efforts to obtain such a charter began in 1722 and were not crowned with success until 1739. Ruth McClure, the historian of the Foundling Hospital in the eighteenth century, attributes the difficulties and delays to the fact that Coram was attempting what had never been attempted before: the application of the principles of the joint stock company to a philanthropic venture. She describes the Foundling Hospital as 'the world's first secular associational philanthropic corporation'.[15] That was not quite true as the establishment of the Westminster and St George's Hospitals on the same principle ante-dated the Foundling by a few years, but that does not detract from the magnitude of Coram's achievement. A hospital for destitute children, or orphanage as we would say, which would be run by private citizens, was a novelty. No one really knew how it would work, so Coram was starting from scratch. As the subsequent history of the Hospital proved, he was remarkably astute in putting together what was to become one of the favourite charities of Londoners, and an ornament to the capital.

In other European countries orphanages were run by the church or the state. According to Ruth McClure:

> ... the former wanted souls, the latter soldiers. In Catholic countries there existed, of course, the desire to combat Protestantism by increasing Church membership ... From the point of view of the Continental state, foundlings as potential soldiers and colonists seemed a good investment. Louis XIV, in his Edict of 1670, made the point precisely in stating why he and his father had made grants to support such children. They had done so 'considering how advantageous their preservation really was, since some of them might become soldiers, and be useful in Our Armies or Troups, some to be Tradesmen, or Inhabitants in Our Colonys, which we are settling for the advantage of the Trade of Our Kingdome'. While the British shared the mercantilist view implicit in the King's statement, they had little interest in maintaining a large standing army.[16]

Ruth McClure cited a pamphlet produced by Dr Bray in support of Coram's long campaign for his Royal Charter which consists of what was to become a familiar mixture in philanthropic literature of appeals to conscience backed up by self-interest:

> First, he urged the Christian duty of saving the lives of innocent children, but in the second place, he pointed out that the children so preserved and properly trained up would not only tend to lower parish rates but also 'will be every one of them rendered useful and fit for Services, and Apprentice-ships to the meanest Trades, instead of being inured to Beggary, Pilfering and Stealing'.[17]

It is impossible to know the extent to which Coram and his helpers were motivated by religious faith. Coram was certainly a Christian, but, at a time when almost everyone described themselves as Christian, it is hard to tell if professions of faith were sincere or simply polite form. The Hospital was a Protestant foundation, of which the staff were required to be Protestants and the foundlings could only be apprenticed to Protestant masters, but this was probably little more than a convention at a time of intense anti-Catholic feeling. Most significantly, there was no requirement for governors of the hospital to take any oath or test, which made it possible to invite Jews and Dissenters to become governors. This was of immense importance as it allowed the Hospital to benefit from the support of wealthy figures in the City who owed no allegiance to the Church of England.[18]

Coram was certainly not an evangelical philanthropist in the mould of the great Victorians like Lord Shaftesbury and Thomas Barnardo, and, if we can jump ahead slightly, it is interesting to compare Barnardo's approach to child care with Coram's. For Barnardo saving children's bodies was but the necessary preliminary to saving their souls, on the grounds that they could not live Christian lives while starvation tempted them into crime. Coram appears to have had no such compelling focus on the next life: he was concerned with saving destitute children for this world. That is not to say that he was irreligious, but he was probably motivated more by his own generous and humane instincts than by any passionate religious conviction. It seems that religious instruction at the Hospital may not have been pursued with any great vigour, and in 1757 Samuel Johnson wrote a piece for the *Literary Magazine* in which he complained that the Foundling children he had spoken to were ignorant of the creed and the commandments.[19]

When seeking his Charter, Coram approached anyone he could get to who might be of assistance to the project, and the Hospital eventually opened with over 170 governors. The type of men whom he approached gives us a reasonable idea of the way in which Coram saw the project as functioning. His governors included dukes and earls, Sir Robert and Horace Walpole, Henry Pelham, the artist William Hogarth, merchants and financiers from the City and some of the leading medical practitioners and professional men of the time. The concentration of wealth and power which these men represented was to stand the Foundling Hospital in good stead, particularly in the City where it became a favourite charity. Most strikingly, however, the list of governors contained almost no churchmen. The Archbishops of Canterbury and York and the Bishop of London were governors *ex officio*, but no other clergymen appeared in the list, even though Coram numbered several amongst his closest friends. We must assume that their absence represented a policy decision on Coram's part to make the Foundling a secular institution, independent of both church and state, unlike any of its continental counterparts.

The great success of the Foundling Hospital revealed the wisdom of Coram's patient work throughout the 17 years of planning. The Hospital opened initially in a house in Hatton Garden, but funds soon became available for a purpose-built structure. The governors paid the Earl of Salisbury £6,500 for fifty-six acres of open land near Lamb's Conduit Street on which they built the Hospital which was to become a London landmark for the next two centuries. The appeal of the Hospital to Londoners was immense. William Hogarth, one of the original governors, took it upon himself to persuade the artists of the day to regard it as a national gallery, and to donate their work. The Hospital soon built up a magnificent collection of works of art, including contributions from Gainsborough, Ramsay, Hayman, Rysbrack and Hogarth himself, who painted Coram's portrait. The Chapel, which opened in 1753, acquired a reputation for its excellent music. Handel, another governor, donated the organ and took a great personal interest in the musical affairs of the Hospital. He conducted or supervised annual public performances of *The Messiah* in the Chapel from 1750 until his death in 1759, and the concerts continued as an annual fundraising event until 1777, by which time they had raised over £9,000. The Chapel became such a fashionable place of worship that the governors were able to charge pew-rents of a guinea per person per annum, with seats in the galleries going for 8 shillings per annum. Coram's policy of asking professional men to become governors also paid dividends. His foundlings enjoyed the medical attention of some of the most fashionable and expensive doctors in eighteenth century London, including Sir Hans Sloane and Sir Richard Mead, who gave their services free. Mead was in the habit of refusing to meet any but grandest of his patients, prescribing for others through an apothecary, but he used to arrive at the Hospital in a gilt coach drawn by six horses to examine urchins who, in some cases, had been literally taken from the gutter.

Altogether the Hospital provided an impressive example of what humanitarian sentiments could achieve when mixed with a keen appreciation of the financial, political, social, artistic and fashionable interests of the age.

'Overrun with Philanthropy'

The nineteenth century was the great age of philanthropy. Even the briefest over-view of its charitable endeavours must leave the modern reader with a sense of exhaustion and inadequacy. There appeared to be no need which could not be met by a group of benevolent citizens, with a chairman and a treasurer, an appeal through the newspapers, some public meetings and a bazaar. There were charities for the poor, for the disabled, for soldiers and sailors, for the reclamation of prostitutes and drunkards, for saving drowning persons, for the provision of medical services, for the unemployed, for working men and apprentices, for shopgirls, for the reformation of housing, for cabbies, costermongers and variety artistes.

'For the cure of every sorrow ... there are patrons, vice-presidents and secretaries,' wrote the historian Sir James Stephen in 1849. 'For the diffusion of every blessing ... there is a committee'.[20]

'We are just now overrun with philanthropy, and God knows where it will stop, or whither it will lead us', said the diarist Charles Greville.[21] If he could be so sour about it in the early part of the nineteenth century, it is difficult to imagine what his reaction would have been towards the end of the century, by which time philanthropy had become a national obsession. A survey conducted in the 1890s found that the average middle-class family devoted ten per cent of its income to philanthropic works, a larger share than that for any other item except food,[22] and a totting-up of the receipts for London charities alone in the mid-1880s enabled *The Times* to announce that they came to more than the entire income of the governments of several European nations.[23] By this stage it was estimated that half a million women worked as full-time volunteers in charities, assisted by another 20,000 who were paid.[24] Charities, including the voluntary hospitals, employed twice as many people as the Poor Law boards, and even at the beginning of the twentieth century charitable incomes, not including church collections, far exceeded government expenditures on the relief of poverty.[25]

The charitable explosion of the nineteenth century is sometimes explained in terms of vast resources confronting vast needs. Rapid industrialisation had changed long-established lifestyles completely in less than a generation. Population growth, coupled with urbanisation, created problems of over-crowding and squalor such as had never been witnessed before. Thousands of poor people were living in conditions more appropriate to animals than human beings. At the same time, the British economy was becoming the largest in the world, and was soon to achieve dominance of the word trading system. Vast personal wealth, coupled with a strict *laissez-faire* doctrine of limited government, meant that private citizens had to address social problems themselves through philanthropy if they wished to prevent the expansion of the state into these areas.

However, this determinist view leaves out the important question of motive. Why should the rich care about the poor? It is not difficult to find examples throughout history of societies in which fabulous wealth has existed alongside dire poverty, without resulting in any great interest in philanthropy.

The Evangelical Impulse

The motivating factor which propelled the charitable bandwagon was a deep religious faith and, in particular, the great evangelical revival which began towards the end of the eighteenth the century. Men like William Wilberforce and John Wesley rejected the Calvinist doctrine of predestination in favour of a view of salvation based upon the individual's rejection of sin and turning to God. This meant addressing poverty, unemployment and lack of education, since these often gave rise to, or were the result of, personal moral failings such as alcoholism, idleness, criminal activity and neglect of hearth and home. Philanthropic work thus took on an eschatological urgency for evangelical Christians: men would go to Hell unless the philanthropists did something to turn them from their wicked ways, and they themselves would go to Hell if they neglected to do everything in their power to save sinners. According to Frank Prochaska:

> In religious diary after diary, good works follow closely upon spiritual vacillation, an immediate, deeply felt struggle with Satan. They were stored up against the Day of Judgement.[26]

In her book *Evangelicals in Action* Kathleen Heasman demonstrated that a vast portion of the whole nineteenth century philanthropic enterprise, comprising, in her estimation, three quarters of all voluntary organisations operating in the second half of the nineteenth century, was run by evangelical Christians.[27] As David Owen, the historian of English philanthropy put it:

> British philanthropy, like Victorian society as whole, became tinctured with the evangelical spirit ... So unwearied in well-doing were certain groups of Bible Christians that in the public mind the word 'philanthropist' became all but synonymous with 'evangelical', and 'philanthropy' was applied to the good works that appealed most to evangelical tastes.[28]

Evangelical, in this context, refers not to a particular denomination, but to a firm belief in salvation by faith alone and in the absolute truthfulness and saving power of the scriptures. Evangelicals might be members of the Church of England, like the Earl of Shaftesbury; they might belong to one of a number of non-conformist denominations; or they might belong to no church at all, like William Booth and Thomas Barnardo who effectively ran their own churches. Evangelical philanthropy, therefore, often took on an ecumenical perspective, bringing together members of different sects in the relief of suffering, although most Evangelicals would have drawn the line at working with Roman Catholics.

A relatively small group of key people were involved in a large number of philanthropic bodies. There were upper class families like the Aberdeens and the Waldegraves, middle class families like the Bevans, the Barclays and the Trittons (all bankers) and businessmen like the Corys, Cardiff shipbuilders, and William Palmer the biscuit manufacturer. These people met each other both socially and professionally, in particular at the series of 'May Meetings' which took place, often at the Exeter Hall in the Strand, when the different organisations would hold their AGMs and prizegivings.

The dedication and inter-connectedness of these Evangelical philanthropists enabled them to exert an influence far beyond their numbers. For example, within the Church of England the Evangelicals constituted only a small faction for most of the nineteenth century, in spite of Lord Shaftesbury's attempts to get Evangelicals appointed to vacant bishoprics. However, it would be a mistake to see the phenomenon of Evangelical philanthropy as the creation of a few wealthy people. Some of the most active and dedicated philanthropists were possessed of only very modest means, like Shaftesbury himself who struggled with debt throughout his life. The funding for the operations came, not in a small number of large donations, but in a large number of small donations. Appeals were launched in Evangelical papers like *The Christian*, and most societies operated their own subscription lists. Kathleen Heasman made the point that, operating in a competitive environment for funds, charities were stimulated by market forces:

> As in the business world, free competition tended to sort out the good from the bad, those organisations which showed reasonable results in relation to the amount subscribed being likely to gain further support, and those performing relatively little tending to disappear.[29]

It was the need to be always trying out new approaches, to see which would work most effectively, which gave these private charities their greatest advantage over blanket systems of state welfare. They were able to initiate new approaches which could be quickly abandoned if they were unsuccessful, or expanded to meet a growing demand. It was within the sphere of the evangelical charities that social work was first developed as a profession,[30] together with the idea that training was necessary for both professional and voluntary charity workers.

Within this process of trial and error charities were able to grow organically from very small to very large organisations, without the stultifying influence of any master plan. After meeting the most obvious needs they could then look for the underlying causes of the problem which also had to be addressed.

From Field Lane to Regent Street

A good example of this was the Field Lane Institution. It began in 1841 as a ragged school, that is to say, a school for the poorest, dirtiest and most disadvantaged children who would not have been admitted to other charitable schools. The original intention for the ragged school, which was established in Caroline Court, off Field Lane, was to operate in the evenings, but this was not a success, so the school became a Sunday School for fifty children. An appeal in *The Times* attracted the attention of Lord Shaftesbury, who became its president, and Charles Dickens, who wrote about it. In 1847 it became a free day school with a paid teacher and seventy pupils.

> The next step was a boys' refuge where the homeless lads slept in a dormitory and were taught tailoring and shoemaking. This was followed by the opening of refuges for homeless men and women, the ragged church, and an adult evening school. The building of the Smithfield market in 1861 meant the removal to new and larger premises, and there more specialised services could be started. These included a day nursery for babies whose mothers were at work, an infant school, industrial schools for boys and for

girls, and a training home for girls who were going into domestic service. Then once again in 1877 a move had to be made and this time the present buildings were erected in Vine Street and opened by Lord Shaftesbury. Here most of the existing activities were continued, and a working boys' hostel and a youths' institute were added. By the 1880's it had become a model institution, with huge Sunday and evening schools and the largest mothers' meeting in London.[31]

Another success story was Quintin Hogg's Youths' Christian Institute, which became the Regent Street Polytechnic, now the University of Westminster. On the basis of his experience with the ragged schools Hogg realised that poor young men needed more than bible studies to equip them for work. He therefore started to hold classes in building and other technical subjects at the ragged school in Longacre between 7.00 am and 8.00 am. They cost one penny, including breakfast, after which the young men could go to their day jobs. Hogg soon needed larger premises, and in 1882 moved to the site in Regent Street. Within twelve months 5,000 students were attending classes in 100 subjects, paying between two shillings and sixpence and four shillings for courses of seven months. Day classes were added to the early morning and evening classes, for girls as well as boys. Polytechnic Holiday Tours took poor young people on overseas trips, while football, cycling, rowing and cricket clubs and a gymnasium took care of the physical wellbeing of students. Furthermore, the students were not allowed to forget their obligations to others less fortunate than themselves. They ran their own mission for the poor, a club and a holiday fund for street boys .[32]

In our own day, when even the smallest local charities demand public money for carrying out quite modest ventures, it is almost impossible to conceive of projects on this scale being carried out by committees of volunteers, dependent on voluntary donations. However the inspiration for these magnificent philanthropies must sound even more bizarre to the modern ear than the financing. As T.H. Pelham, the early historian of the Regent Street Polytechnic, explained:

> The public did not understand that the real secret of success from the beginning was the Sunday afternoon Bible class, which formed a bond of union and Christian fellowship for those engaged in working the various departments of the Institute. Q.H.[Quintin Hogg] used often to say that quite apart from the direct spiritual results the Bible class was the keystone of success for all boys' clubs and institutes.[33]

As we shall see later, the great Victorian philanthropists were united on this point. They felt that material assistance on its own was worthless unless it was accompanied by a concern for the moral and spiritual needs of the recipient. Indeed it was the spiritual welfare of the needy which was the primary concern. As Rev Thomas Chalmers put it in 1819: 'I should count the Salvation of a single soul of more value than the deliverance of a whole empire from pauperism'—and he was a man who cared passionately about pauperism.[34]

Eminent Philanthropists

The Poor Man's Earl

O F ALL the evangelical philanthropists none was greater than Lord Shaftesbury. Anthony Ashley-Cooper, who became the seventh Earl of Shaftesbury in 1851,[1] was regarded as the leading evangelical Christian, and many would have said the leading Christian, of his time. He became, like Wilberforce before him, as a sort of conscience to the nation, a man of such outstanding virtue that the association of his name with any enterprise gave it instant respectability and mass appeal. He was, tragically, subject to severe depression throughout his life, which coloured his view of other people and the way in which they regarded him. 'I may be loved in Bethnal Green but I am despised in Belgravia'[2] was one of the many gloomy reflections in his diary, and this was written in 1881 when his public image was heroic. Prime Ministers had tried throughout his life to get him to hold office in their governments, knowing that his participation would raise the tone of any administration, but he almost always refused, whilst at the same time complaining bitterly that he was not appreciated.

He was more co-operative with philanthropic bodies, becoming the founder, patron or president of so many voluntary organisations that nearly 200 were represented at his funeral. Nor was he the sort of patron who allows his name to be used on the letterhead and then does nothing else. He attended meetings with scrupulous regularity, he made suggestions and then carried them through, and he used his position in parliament and in society to further the aims of any project he was committed to. What makes this all the more extraordinary is that Shaftesbury was never a wealthy man, and was unable to afford secretarial assistance. He was consequently left with the burden of maintaining an immense hand-written correspondence on top of everything else.

He entered parliament in 1826 as Conservative member for Woodstock and held the seat until 1846 when he resigned as a result of differences with his constituents over the Corn Laws. (The farmers wanted to retain them but he accepted that they had to go.) He was out of parliament for only a few months until he was elected as Conservative member for Bath in 1847, a seat he held until he entered the House of Lords on his father's death in 1851.

He will always be remembered for the legislation which he promoted to prevent the exploitation of women and children in mines and factories, and it has been customary to regard Shaftesbury as having inherited the mantle of William Wilberforce and the so-called Clapham Sect. This small group of fervent evangelicals used to meet in Henry Thornton's house in Clapham where, amongst other things, they planned their great campaign against slavery. The methods which they pioneered became the stock-in-trade of pressure groups down to our own day, and the great Acts of 1807 (which banned slave trading) and 1832 (which freed the slaves and compensated their masters) stand as milestones of selfless and enlightened political activism.

Like Wilberforce, who was more than forty years his senior, Shaftesbury was a lifelong parliamentarian who put his conscience before considerations of party and career. However, the scope of his reforming zeal was much broader than that of the older man. Although Wilberforce was involved in a minor way with movements for prison and agricultural reform and for the relief of poverty, he regarded the abolition of the slave trade as 'the grand object of my Parliamentary existence'[3], besides which his other activities were insignificant. Shaftesbury took a wider view. He wanted men and women to be free from the sort of oppressive circumstances which prevented them from living decent and fulfilled lives, and this took him into areas where members of the Clapham Sect would not have dreamt of going, like the slums and the cesspits of the East End of London.

The Lunacy Laws

The first of Shaftesbury's great causes, and the one at which he laboured for the longest period, was the reform of the lunacy laws. At the beginning of the nineteenth century the treatment of lunatics was so savage that, in the worst cases, mentally ill people were being kept in conditions which no farmer would have tolerated for his animals, permanently chained in filth and darkness. Pauper lunatics were confined to the workhouse, but the mentally ill of prosperous families, who were kept in private asylums, were sometimes even worse off. This was particularly true if the inheritance of property was involved, and the death of the confined party eagerly awaited. The worst horrors concerned sane people who were confined as lunatics by unscrupulous relatives.

Within less than a year of his entering parliament, Shaftesbury was asked to sit on a Select Committee 'On Pauper Lunatics in the County of Middlesex and on Lunatic Asylums'. As a result of this committee's report on the terrible maltreatment of lunatics two Acts of Parliament were passed in 1828 which, among other things, made the Home Secretary responsible for the inspection and licensing of all lunatic asylums, public and private. The inspections were to be carried out by committees of magistrates in the provinces and by a fifteen-member Metropolitan Lunacy Commission in London, with Shaftesbury as one of the Commissioners. In 1829 he became its Chairman, and in the 1840s its remit was extended to the whole country. In 1845 Shaftesbury was appointed permanent chairman, a position he retained until his death. He was responsible for many improvements in the treatment of the mentally ill, including an Act of 1845 which compelled every county authority to erect asylums, and came to be regarded as the greatest living expert on the issue. He was still haranguing the House of Lords about it in 1884, the year before his death.

Shaftesbury and the Board of Health

Shaftesbury's interest in public health was first aroused by Edwin Chadwick's 1842 *Report on the Sanitary Condition of the Labouring Population of Great Britain*. He supported several voluntary organisations which addressed health issues, like the Association for Promoting Cleanliness Among the Poor, and when a Board of Health was established in 1848 he agreed to become an unpaid commissioner.

The Board's remit was to concern itself with what seem to us the very obvious public health issues of drainage, drinking water and sewerage, but at the time these were not regarded as the province of government. There was intense opposition, not only from the Treasury, which resisted this extension of the realm of government for fiscal reasons, but from all sections of the political nation, including the press, who saw the Board's plans for large-scale public works as a threat to private property. Set up in the year of a major cholera epidemic, the Board was given certain powers to order the cleansing of filthy alleys and tenements, and to carry out house-to-house visiting to track down cases for early treatment. However, as the epidemic died away, so did the very modest enthusiasm for public health measures. After several years of tortuous political manoeuvring the Board was closed down in 1854, having achieved very little in terms of practical improvements. The only legislation which Shaftesbury was able to promote in the area was an 1851 Act for the regulation and inspection of lodging houses, which brought what were often vermin-infested slums under the control of local authorities by a system of licensing, and opened them to inspection by the police and medical authorities. The Act was described by Charles Dickens (who was no friend of Shaftesbury's) as 'the best law...ever passed by an English parliament',[4] and it resulted in a decline in disease and crime, but it was hardly on a par with the supply of clean drinking water to London, which the Board was aiming for.

However, in the opinion of his biographer G.F.A. Best, Shaftesbury's work in public health was second only to his reform of the lunacy laws amongst his great works:

> ... while the General Board of Health survived, it accomplished great things. It laid the foundations of British public health; it established a network of local health authorities for subsequent legislators and administrators ... to improve and extend; ... it began that accumulation of expert knowledge, that process of continuous research and enquiry, which was and always must be prerequisite to any effective system of social welfare.[5]

Perhaps of equal significance, however, was Shaftesbury's association of Christian charity with questions of housing and public health. We now take this sort of concern for granted, but it was a novelty in the mid-nineteenth century. The earlier generation of Evangelical campaigners for social reform, like Wilberforce and Elizabeth Fry, had shown no interest in such questions as they were not regarded as having a spiritual dimension. For Shaftesbury, however, anything which stood between the individual and the possibility of living the sort of decent life which would lead to salvation had to be tackled. As Georgina Battiscombe put it:

> He saw clearly that people obliged to live in sub-human conditions could not be expected to live ... according to the super-human standards demanded of Christians. He knew, for instance, that it was useless to preach chastity to boys and girls living in overcrowded cottages and forced to sleep side-by-side in the same room.[6]

In the area of public health, as with everything he did, Shaftesbury's aims were spiritual. His intention was to Christianize the condition of the working classes,[7] and if that meant leaving his mansion in Grosvenor Square to peer into the sewers of Southwark and Bermondsey, then that was what he would do. Modern admirers of the campaigning Earl tend to concentrate on his reforms while neglecting his motives, but this is to misrepresent him in a most fundamental way. When he agreed to joint the Board of Health he wrote to Lord Morpeth:

> I shall humbly and heartily pray to Almighty God that it may please Him, for the sake of our blessed Redeemer, to prosper this work to the glory of His own name, and the permanent welfare of our beloved Country.[8]

This may seem to us a faintly ridiculous way in which to be talking about drains,[9] but that reaction tells us as much about our own priorities as Shaftesbury's.

Perhaps nothing sets his welfare campaigns in perspective so clearly as the course of action he adopted when he inherited the earldom in 1851. He found his estate neglected, dilapidated and insanitary. His tenants and labourers were living in such squalid accommodation that, as his political opponents did not hesitate to point out, the mill-hands in Lancashire, whose champion he had become through his factory acts, enjoyed a higher standard of living than those who depended directly in him. Shaftesbury felt this criticism keenly and wanted to rebuild his mouldering cottages, but he found the estate so encumbered with debt that it was extremely difficult to find the money for even the smallest improvements. Nevertheless, the first thing he undertook was to re-order the interior of the church, which he said looked too much like a ballroom, and to employ a scripture reader, whose salary was an additional burden. He also ordered the tap-room on the estate to close at nine o'clock. Religion and morals came before physical well-being. Without such passionately held beliefs, issues of social reform would have held no interest for him.

Reform in the Factories

The legal reforms with which Shaftesbury's name is most often associated are those relating to the regulation of labour. Throughout his life he campaigned ceaselessly to protect workers, particularly women and children, from exploitive conditions, whether in factories, down mines or up chimneys. The history of the many acts of parliament which Shaftesbury either introduced or promoted or inspired is a long one, and has been told many times by his biographers. He was able to stop women and children from being sent down the mines, to shorten the working day and provide time for the education of factory children, to stop small boys from being sent up chimneys, and to establish inspectorates on which all future regulation of factory and mine labour depended.

His fame as a reforming parliamentarian has tended to give the impression that he saw the political arena as the source of social welfare, but this was far from being the case. Like most of the Victorian philanthropists Shaftesbury made a firm distinction between what belonged in the political realm and what was the responsibility of private citizens. He gave a clear demonstration of this when he was asked for support by Rev George Staite, a vicar in Cheshire who was working to establish what was to become the National Society for the Prevention of Cruelty to Children (NSPCC). Shaftesbury replied as follows:

> The evils you state are enormous and indisputable, but they are of so private, internal and domestic a character as to be beyond the reach of legislation. The subject, indeed, would not, I think, be entertained in either House of Parliament.
>
> No laws could command and watch over the detailed and daily duties of mothers to their children. You have a sound principle and a blessed object before you, but you need a machinery for carrying it into execution.
>
> The Institution of the Bible Women such as we have in London for some years past, is precisely the one that would meet your requirements. A Bible Woman gains easier access to the families; her sex disarms much opposition; and her knowledge of all the small items of domestic life, and her will and capacity to give assistance to them, furnishes her with opportunities that no man could obtain.
>
> A Committee of two or three ladies will be quite sufficient to procure the funds necessary for her maintenance, and to superintend her operations.
>
> The results from our efforts in London are most satisfactory. We have, in daily activity, full two hundred of these admirable agents, and I believe that under God's blessing, their presence is better than all the laws that could be framed.[10]

Shaftesbury was opposed to legislation to criminalise child abuse, even though he had such a horror of it that it caused him uncharacteristically to question divine providence: 'Why such parents are allowed to have offspring; why to exercise such power? ... All these are thoughts full of distress and difficulty', he wrote in his diary.[11] However, he felt that the intrusion of the state into the home would be both ineffective and undesirable, and that the personal approach by Christian social workers would be preferable. This may seem an extreme position to us now, and Shaftesbury did in fact relent to the extent of becoming President of the newly-formed London Society for the Prevention of Cruelty to Children,[12] and making his last speech to its first annual meeting. However, a series of scandals over a century later in the 1980s and 1990s, in which dozens of children were taken from their homes by police and social workers, sometimes in dramatic 'dawn raids', only to be returned after months or even years when no evidence of abuse could be found, vindicated Shaftesbury's caution about invoking the powers of the state in domestic affairs.

Ragged Religion

Of all his philanthropic works, none gave Shaftesbury more pleasure than the ragged schools. These were voluntary establishments which provided a very basic education for children who were too dirty and ill-disciplined to attend even the other charity schools which catered for the poor. They were all religiously inspired, covering every shade of denominationalism from Tractarian to Unitarian, and placed more emphasis on religious than secular subjects. By seeking to educate the children who were, so to speak, at the bottom of the heap, the schools made a great difference, not only to the pupils, for whom the alternative would have been no education at all, but to the cities they lived in. The fall in crime rates in Victorian England, which many historians have commented on,[13] is at least partly attributable to the success of the ragged schools.

In 1844 the Ragged Schools Union was formed to make the movement more coherent and effective, with Shaftesbury as President. He threw himself into it with his usual commitment but with more than usual pleasure, as the work appealed to his great love of children.[14] The annual May meetings of the RSU, held at Exeter Hall in the Strand, were amongst the happiest of his year. Before a packed audience of teachers and subscribers, Shaftesbury would award good conduct prizes to nearly one thousand pupils. 'If the Ragged School system were to fail', he once wrote, 'I should not die in the course of nature, I should die of a broken heart'.[15] Whether or not his death was the result of a broken heart, Shaftesbury lived to see the ragged schools fail, not from lack of public support, but as the direct result of government action. A growing feeling that education was a vital precondition for a fulfilling and productive life led to the view that the state should provide it. Gladstone managed to overcome his reluctance to augment the state sector by persuading himself that education was a special case, and in 1870 W.E. Forster, the President of his Board of Education, introduced the Education Act which sought to provide universal access to schooling. It did not take over or interfere with the existing charitable schools, but it set up school boards, with the power to levy a local rate, to build Board schools where there was no charitable provision.

Shaftesbury perceived immediately the danger which a state system of education would pose to the voluntary sector, and particularly to Christian education. He had always maintained that 'religion must be the alpha and omega of all education given to the poorer classes',[16] but where would religious education be under a state system? Although it was agreed that religious education must form part of the curriculum in state schools, a bitter argument broke out between the different churches over exactly what should be taught. The established church and the nonconformists both suspected that their rivals would high-jack the system for sectarian ends, so, in order to keep the peace, an amendment was introduced by Shaftesbury's brother-in-law, William Cowper-Temple, which provided for Biblical teaching in every Board school, but not according to the formularies of any one denomination. Shaftesbury realised that such a milk-and-water approach to religion would amount to little. He remarked that: 'Though thinking people might complain of what was left out' of religious teaching in Board schools, 'no living soul could make a grievance of what was left in... Ten thousand are taught to read, not one hundred will be taught to know that there is a God'.[17]

Shaftesbury voted for the Bill because he suspected that, if it failed, it would be followed by another which would ban religious teaching in state schools altogether, but he was deeply unhappy with it. 'Well, the Education Bill is passed', he wrote to Cowper-Temple; 'It was inevitable; but you will date, from it, the greatest moral change that England has ever known'.[18] Given the apparent impossibility of enforcing even the minimal legal provisions for religious education within state schools,[19] who can doubt that Shaftesbury was right to doubt that a state-run education system would remain Christian in any but the most nominal sense?

Voluntarism and the State

The Education Act 1870 was not like the National Health Act 1946. It did not seek deliberately to wipe out a large area of voluntary activity and replace it with a state monopoly. On the contrary, the government wanted the voluntary school movement to continue: the expense of replacing these schools or taking them over would have been immense.

However, the funds and the enthusiasm for voluntary schools began to dry up when the public realised that the state had accepted responsibility for education, and the ragged schools were the first to collapse. 'Ragged Schools fell rapidly and like ninepins', Shaftesbury later recalled, 'the very instant it was declared that the State intended to meddle with Education and substitute the compulsory for the voluntary principle'.[20]

The Father of Nobody's Children

In 1872 Shaftesbury held a meeting at his house in Grosvenor Square for a group of fourteen or fifteen evangelists who were working in the East End. His intention was to learn more about their work and to encourage co-operation between the different organisations, but he was not seeking to persuade them to merge or give up particular functions:

It is evident that there are several thousand people who would be destitute of all spiritual care and as lost as the tribes at the centre of Africa but for the agencies represented here. Possibly something may be done to tighten the bands that bind you, but I should be sorry for anything to hinder your individual and independent action.[21]

Amongst the guests was Thomas Barnardo, a 27-year old missionary who had arrived in London from Dublin six years previously. Brought up as an unenthusiastic member of the established Church of Ireland, Barnardo had become what we would call a born-again Christian as a teenager and joined the Plymouth Brethren. He conceived a passion for missionary work in China, and came to London in 1866 to join the China Inland Mission.

However, his enthusiasm for saving Chinese souls received only a cautious welcome from the Mission. Barnardo had certain personality defects which made him a bad bet for anyone organising a team ministry. He was arrogant and intolerant of any form of authority, being temperamentally unable to submit himself to any sort of external discipline. The Mission advised him to find something else to do for a while they considered his application.

Balked of his intended Chinese converts, Barnardo joined the growing throng of missionaries who were already preaching in the East End of London, an area characterised, as some of them were fond of pointing out, by a degree of heathenism which rivalled that of the African jungle. He also began teaching in a ragged school and, after (inevitably) falling out with the committee which ran it, he started his own. Calling it the East End Juvenile Mission, Barnardo opened his ragged school in Hope Place in 1868. Like other promoters of the ragged schools, his aims were as much evangelical as educational. He saw it as his role to prepare the children for heaven by saving them from lives of sin and crime.

The work of saving waifs and strays from the street, for which he was to become famous, began slightly later. Because Barnardo was so prone to embellish the events of his own life in order to imbue them with the legendary status, it is always difficult to establish the facts, and particularly the dates, of key events.[22] However it seems that at some time in the winter of 1869/70 he had his fateful conversation with a boy called Jim Jarvis. Jarvis was unwilling to leave the ragged school at the end of the day, and asked to be allowed to sleep on the floor in front of the fire. Barnardo told him he must go home and had difficulty in believing that the boy literally had no home to go to. He took Jarvis back to his own room and was inclined to disbelieve his story about the homeless boys who slept rough in London, so they set off after midnight for a trip to one of the 'lays', where they found eleven small boys sleeping on the iron roof of a shed in the freezing cold. It was this experience which set Barnardo off on his lifelong crusade to shelter destitute children.

Barnardo opened his first refuge for homeless boys in 1870, and in his report for the East End Juvenile Mission of 1870/1 he announced that he was caring for 33 boys there. It was in the same year that he was told that he would definitely not be accepted by the China Inland Mission. From that time on he regarded himself as divinely appointed to the care of homeless children.

Shortly after this (again, the date is uncertain) Barnardo had the second of the legendary encounters which were to affect his life's work. Whilst on one of his night-time rambles in search of destitute children he came upon an unusually large group in Billingsgate. One of the boys, John Somers, known as Carrots because of his red hair, pleaded for admission into the refuge, but Barnardo only had five places and said he would have to wait for a vacancy. Shortly afterwards Carrots was found dead from starvation and hypothermia at the age of eleven. Barnardo was so mortified that he had refused the child that he adopted an open-door policy. 'No destitute boy ever refused admission' was painted on the door of every refuge, to be changed to 'No destitute child ever refused admission' after the opening of the Girls' Village Home. He made absolutely no distinction on grounds of age, race, sex, religion or disability: he only had to be convinced that the need was genuine.

Nor did he remain confined to the capital. His East End Juvenile Mission soon expanded out of the East End and out of London. He opened receiving centres called Ever Open Doors in fourteen major cities, each of which was capable of accommodating up to fifteen children while their needs were being assessed. He had thus committed himself to proving a national childcare service for destitute children with nothing to rely on apart from the voluntary contributions of donors.

Although, like other great campaigners for social reform, Barnardo liked to make out that he was the first and only figure in the field, there were other charities dealing with destitute children before his. What set him apart from his rivals—and there is little doubt that he regarded them in that light—was the scale and the quality of his operation. His open-door policy soon made him responsible for the welfare of hundreds, and then thousands of children. By the time of his death over 60,000 children had passed through his homes. The fact that the operation remained afloat at all was due to his combination of profound faith in his mission, which resulted in a determination to face down all obstacles, coupled with a genius for both administration and publicity—a rare combination.

He was a marketing man and fundraiser before charities used such terms. He was the first to use photography for fundraising purposes, selling packs of 'before' and 'after' pictures of the 'saved' children. He instigated a national street collection (Waif Saturday) and organised house-to-house collections, using volunteers to leave envelopes for collection later. He staged massive spectacles at the Albert Hall, involving parades and demonstrations by the children, including a 'cripples' cricket match', and he even turned his birthday into a major annual fundraising event. In the course of his lifetime he raised something like £3 million, but the money was always going out faster than it came in.

However, it was not just quantity that mattered to Barnardo, but the quality of care which was given to the children. Barnardo was motivated by a genuine love of children, and was sincere when he said:

> I always ask myself when I have to deal with children committed to my care, what would I do in such a case if the child were my own daughter.[23]

He was outstanding amongst the philanthropists of his time in his willingness to take on physically and mentally disabled children, when other children's homes shunned them because of the expense and the open-ended nature of the commitment to people who could never be self supporting.[24] He did a great deal of work to assist single mothers, often arranging for their children to be cared for in homes close to the mother's place of work to enable visiting. This was a risky policy at the time, as he could have been accused of encouraging immorality, and he had been pursuing it for thirteen years before he mentioned it to his donors in 1902.

Most importantly perhaps, he was amongst the first to realise the importance to children of a family atmosphere, and the disadvantages of being brought up in an institution. He set up an elaborate and extensive network of foster-carers, even though it was more difficult to raise funds for this work than for the homes, which had a more obvious appeal. At the time of his death in 1905 Barnardo was responsible for the care of 7,998 children, of whom more than half were boarded out, or fostered, and over 1,300 of whom were disabled.

In 1894 the Local Government Board set up a committee to inquire into the working of Poor Law schools, as well as the work of voluntary institutions in the field of childcare. Several committee members, including Mrs Barnett of Toynbee Hall and the chairman, A.J. Mundella, admitted afterwards that they had been prejudiced against Barnardo to begin with but, after investigation, came to admire his methods. Addressing a public meeting after the publication of the committee's report, Mundella was unstinting in his praise:

> I can only say to you, without in the least flattering Dr Barnardo, that at the conclusion of our enquiry I came to the opinion ... that we could wish that in the Local Government Board there was a department for the Poor Law children of this country ... and that we had a Dr Barnardo to place at the head of them ... Most of the reforms that the Committee has recommended, Dr Barnardo has anticipated ... We found ... that Dr Barnardo was often boarding-out ... more children than the whole of the local authorities of this kingdom ... the sanitary condition of all the children under Dr Barnardo's care is something that is marvellous, in contrast with those under our local and State system.[25]

King of the Castle

At the time of Lord Shaftesbury's meeting, when Barnardo was asked to speak about his work to a group of other evangelists, he was not particularly well known. Although he had opened his first Refuge in 1870, when he went to tea with Lord Shaftesbury in the spring of 1872 he was known, if at all, as just another missionary to the poor of the East End. By the autumn of that year he had achieved a triumph which put him in a different league altogether.

He had been using a 'gospel tent', set up outside a notorious East End gin palace called the Edinburgh Castle, for his revival meetings. When the landlord put up the lease of the pub for sale, at £4,200, Barnardo deployed all of his considerable powers of persuasion to raise the entire sum in time to complete the purchase in October. He then regilded and redecorated the bar, installing gasoliers to make it even more glitzy, and opened it as a 'British workman's coffee palace'. It had bars, a library, reading and smoking room, and aimed to provide comfortable relaxation for working people without the sale of the demon drink. The opening ceremony was performed by Lord Shaftesbury, and the whole thing was a triumph which had people comparing Barnardo with William Booth as a great evangelist.

The Edinburgh Castle was much more than a non-alcoholic pub: it was to become Barnardo's church—or cathedral. The great hall was his mission church and he was the pastor, unallied to any denomination, preaching the gospel as he saw fit, to a congregation which ran into thousands. Barnardo described the ecclesiastical influences as 'eclectic', combining bits of Brethrenism and bits of Quakerism, but the most important influence was Barnardoism. He was running an independent church.

To Barnardo himself, and to some of his contemporaries, his role as pastor of the Edinburgh Castle was amongst the most important of his achievements. After his death he lay in state there. However the fame of Dr Barnardo of Barnardo's Homes reached such proportions that people began to forget that the Father of Nobody's Children was, first and foremost, a missionary seeking to save souls.

This was the perspective he brought to bear on his work with the children. 'My heart's desire and prayer to God for the children is that they might be saved, not only for the present life but for the life to come',[26] he wrote. The relief of physical suffering and material want was of little account compared with the children's eternal salvation, and without this spiritual imperative the work would have held no appeal for him. The work of Barnardo's Homes had two main thrusts: to train the children to be useful and productive members of society, and to be faithful and devout Christians. His boys and girls learnt at an early age both the importance of work, and the need to raise funds to pay for the running of the organisation which was caring for them. The first of his operations was a City Messenger Service. 'The accurate and careful delivery of TRADE CIRCULARS and other PUBLIC NOTICES cannot be achieved in a more economical or satisfactory way', Barnardo assured his customers. This was followed by a woodchopping brigade, shoe blacking, brush making, tailoring, training for domestic service and other skills.

Religious education in Barnardo's Homes was not an optional extra but the main point of the whole operation. He described the homes as 'houses of prayer, where war must be waged on ... the heartless principles of secularism',[27] and he put the children's religious upbringing at the very top of his list of priorities. He refused to allow children to go to foster-parents who were not Christians, no matter how respectable they might be, and he would withdraw children from homes in areas in which the vicars were displaying High Church tendencies. His 1899 Christmas message to the boys in his Epsom home was revealing:

> Don't forget your Great Father in Heaven who supplies all His children with such beautiful hands; and don't forget your small father in London who loves you very sincerely.[28]

By juxtaposing himself with God the Father, Barnardo managed to give the impression that he was almost part of the Trinity. He certainly regarded his own work as a barometer of the nation's religious well-being:

> ... it is one of the evidences of Christianity and it is not too much to say that in its success or failure may be seen a gauge of the Christian impulse.[29]

Just how passionately Barnardo felt about the religious welfare of the children under his care was revealed in a series of court cases which took place at the beginning of the 1890s.

Barnardo in Court

Barnardo felt, with all the conviction of a man who sees himself as divinely inspired, that he alone was responsible for the children in his care. He once rebuked a member of staff who had unwisely written to him about one of 'her' children. 'Not yours' he answered, 'she is mine, *mine, mine!*'.[30]

In fact the law gave him no such proprietary rights. Voluntary bodies which had undertaken the care of children had absolutely no legal status of guardianship. The parents could turn up at any time and demand the return of their children, which some of them did when the children became old enough to contribute financially to the household. This was, of course, distressing for the staff of children's homes who knew that, in some cases, they were giving the children back to violent and abusive parents. However, Barnardo was not a man to allow the law to stand in his way. He would invariably refuse to hand back children and, because the parents were usually poor and ill-educated, he could be fairly sure that they would not stand on their legal rights against him.

In 1888 he accepted three children, Hary Gossage, Martha Tye and John Roddy, all of whom were demanded back by their parents in the following year. He refused, as he had refused all such requests, but in this case there was an additional factor: all three children were from Roman Catholic families, and they were being requested, not to live with their admittedly hopeless parents, but to be brought up in Catholic institutions. To Barnardo, whose hatred of the Catholic church verged on the pathological, this was the proverbial red rag. He might still have got away with his refusals to comply, had it not been for the fact that all three parents used the same firm of well-known Catholic solicitors. It seems fairly clear that, at some stage, the Catholic hierarchy became involved, seeing this as a direct threat to the right of parents to have their children educated in the

Catholic faith. Barnardo was up against much more than the demands of ignorant and impoverished parents this time.

The complicated history of the three court cases, which were heard separately, and which stretched over several years, is well told by Gillian Wagner in her classic biography of Barnardo. Briefly, writs of habeas corpus were served on Barnardo for all three children, but he refused to comply. Harry Gossage and Martha Tye had already been sent out of the country before the writs could be served, Harry to Canada and Martha (supposedly) to France. Barnardo claimed to have no addresses for them and to be unable to get the children back. The judges in the Tye case were outraged by Barnardo's behaviour, and one of them described him as 'quite unworthy to be entrusted with ... the care of such large numbers of children if he is capable of acting in such a way as he has acted in this case'.[31] Barnardo, who could never bear to be in the wrong, appealed the cases right up to the House of Lords, but without success. He was in contempt of court for ignoring or refusing to comply with writs of habeas corpus, but in fact the two children were never produced, and nothing more is known of them.

His behaviour in the John Roddy case was actually worse. On this occasion he was not able to get the child out of the country before being served with the writ, so he felt even more passionately about winning the case. He told the Court of Appeal that he had received John Roddy covered in vermin, clothed in rags and looking half-starved. However the child's admission record, which carried the usual photograph and medical report, contradicted this. He was shown as neatly dressed and in good health. When Barnardo presented this record to the Court in evidence he removed both the photograph and the medical report. When he was forced to supply them the judges formed a very critical view of his behaviour. Once again the judgement went against him, and he was described by one of the judges as being 'unfit to have the uncontrolled and absolute power' which he demanded over the child.

Because Barnardo was now fighting three similar cases, and had shown himself determined to take them all to the highest level, both sides then petitioned to have the boy put under the guardianship of a person of standing. The Catholics nominated a Mr Walsh, but Barnardo trumped this by nominating Sir Robert Fowler, a former Lord Mayor or London. The case was heard before the Master of the Rolls, who astutely observed:

> ... this is not a mere dispute between the wife of a labouring man and Dr Barnardo. It is a dispute between two sets of earnest benevolent enthusiasts ... it is a fight over the soul, and not over the body of the child.[32]

This was precisely the reason for Barnardo's dogged determination not to give in. Once again, he took it to the House of Lords and lost. This time he had to hand over the child, and he bitterly reproached himself for cowardice in doing so.

However, by the time of his final defeat in the House of Lords in July 1891 the law relating to the custody of children had been changed.

Barnardo's court appearances highlighted a serious gap in the legal protection of children. It was clearly undesirable that parents, no matter how abusive or neglectful, should be regarded as having such absolute rights over their children as to be able to remove them from institutions into which they had been received for their own protection. In March 1891 the Custody of Children Act gave the courts wide discretionary powers to refuse such applications. It became known as the Barnardo Act.

Barnardo's behaviour throughout the court cases had shown him at his worst. He had obviously developed a taste for litigation. He insisted on representing himself and spent a great deal of time researching the legal background. He spoke at what seemed like interminable length, to the obvious irritation of the judges who struggled to keep him to the point, and everything was complicated by his increasing deafness. He showed himself to be absolutely unwilling to accept any judgement on his own behaviour and to be quite prepared to mislead the court to achieve his ends. He almost certainly perjured himself on a number of occasions. Furthermore, he ran up enormous legal costs which, despite his protestations to the contrary, eventually fell on his organisation. He also lost much support for his work by his arrogant behaviour.

Nevertheless, it is typical of Barnardo that, even when he was showing himself in his worst light, he achieved a victory for children. The Custody of Children Act was one of the earliest pieces of legislation to recognise that parents do not have the right to treat their children just as they wish. As Gillian Wagner observed:

> ... the fight between Barnardo and the Roman Catholics for the right to instruct [the three children] in the Christian faith acted as a catalyst which lit up whole areas where an unjust law could be used against the true interests of children. Perhaps only religious fanaticism could have caused the litigants to go to such lengths.[33]

Barnardo and William Booth

There is a tradition in the Salvation Army that when young Thomas Barnardo came to London in 1866 he was so impressed by the work of William Booth's Christian Mission (which later became the Salvation Army) that he became involved with it. Eventually, realising that his calling was specifically related to working with children, he bade a fond farewell to Booth, who gave him this encouraging benediction: 'You look after the children and I'll look after the adults, then together we'll convert the world'.

This charming story has, unfortunately, no basis in fact and must be filed under 'Myth and Legend'.[34] There is no evidence that Barnardo ever worked in the Christian Mission, and, if the two men ever met, neither of them referred to it. This is all the more strange as they were starting their missionary work in the East End at exactly the same time, and were for a while both preaching from the same patch of waste land on the Mile End Road. However, both Barnardo and Booth were the sort of men who had to keep the spotlight trained on themselves. Others working in the same field were seen as rivals for funds and publicity: they were either ignored or attacked.

After initially welcoming the formation of the Society for Waifs and Strays (which became the Church of England Children's Society, now known as the Children's Society), Barnardo adopted a hostile attitude when he realised that they were competing with him for support. He also resigned from the council of the Society for the Prevention of Cruelty to Children, of which he was founder member, on the ridiculous pretext that Cardinal Manning was using the organisation to spread the insidious snares of the Roman church.

Like Barnardo, William Booth was not the man to give friendly words of encouragement to someone leaving his organisation to set up as a rival. Booth, who was fond of telling his children that he was their General before he was their father, turned bitterly against three of them who had the temerity to 'desert' from the Salvation Army, and would probably have had them court-martialled if he could.

Booth was a man whose need for complete control was such that he abandoned his career as an ordained minister of the Methodist New Connexion because they had forbidden him to work as an itinerant evangelist and tried to tie him down to pastoral duties on a circuit. In order to promote his own vision of Christian engagement with a wicked world he chose to work as an independent—one might say freelance—missioner and came to London in 1865 where he set up the East London Revival Society. This was re-named the East London Christian Mission, then the Christian Mission, and finally in January 1879 it became the Salvation Army, with Booth as it General.[35]

The Bells of Hell

From an early age Booth had become convinced that the majority of mankind was heading straight for hell and that it was his duty to save them. He felt called to go after the lowest and most degenerate sinners of all and to shake them into a realisation of what the love of Christ meant for them. However he recognised that, for those living a life of hot sin, only hot religion would offer an attractive alternative. As a result, his meetings soon became notorious. Loud music, raucous singing, tearful testimonies and hordes of sinners crowding to the penitent-form to be saved created an exciting atmosphere not entirely dissimilar to that of the gin palaces from which he had dragged his audience. He attracted enormous publicity, coupled with a certain amount of professional jealousy on the part of rival Christian missionaries who thought he was poaching souls from them. Even in the noble breast of Lord Shaftesbury there lurked the tiniest suggestion of envy. According to Georgina Battiscombe:

> Shaftesbury first refers to the Salvation Army on September 17th 1879, when he quotes Gamaliel's advice to the Sanhedrin, 'Refrain from these men and let them alone, for if this counsel or this work be of man it will come to

naught, but if it be of God ye cannot overthrow it'. Three years later he was so convinced of the uncelestial origin of the Salvation Army that he described the movement as 'anti-Christian and most perilous'. He, who had once urged Christians to be 'abnormal, eccentric, wild, extravagant, but by every means we must preach Christ to the people', now complained of 'doings ... as extravagant and in expression as offensive, as any that ever disgraced the wildest fanaticism'.[36]

In his defence Booth could say that his extravagance paid off. He reached the sinners who would never have gone near a quiet and respectable mission, and indeed he initially used circuses and theatres for his meetings to dispel the usual gloomy associations of chapels and mission halls. He dealt with people as he found them. He spoke to criminals and degenerates in language they could understand, and when he had converted them he sent them out as missionaries to redeem their own kind. He found his evangelists for the conversion of drunkards in public houses, and sent reformed criminals to stand at prison gates to meet discharged prisoners. A Salvationist who was a former brothel-keeper played a vital part in the campaign to eliminate the white-slave trade which resulted in the Act of Parliament which raised the age of consent to 16.

The Salvation Army pursued an intensely spiritual agenda by means of a down-to-earth approach to practical problems. One degraded sneak-thief who came to the penitent form to be saved presented a tricky problem: he had a tattoo of the Devil over his heart. An image of the Devil was not something the Salvationists would have taken lightly, but removing tattoos in those days was impossible. The solution was to call in a skilled tattooist to transform the Devil into an angel.[37]

It was this mixture of hard-headed realism with intense spiritual fervour which gave the Army its appeal. The posters for one of Booth's early missions advertised the appearance of 'A Milkman Who Has Not Watered His Milk Since He Was Saved',[38] and it seems reasonable to assume that the material advantages of a godly lifestyle meant at least as much to the saved as any theological considerations. 'I can say religion is a good thing', said one converted sinner, 'my body is stronger, my soul is saved, my wife is happier, my children are clothed, my house is better furnished, and, having signed the pledge and given over smoking, I can say, "Godliness is profitable for all things"'.[39] This practicality had its effect upon the benefactors. A Lancashire lawyer, who had promised Booth £100, attended a meeting in Whitechapel, where he sat among the converts. He noticed that they all had clean necks and ears, and raised his donation to £1,000, saying: 'General, yours is a work of practical godliness'.[40] The Baptist preacher Charles Spurgeon maintained that, if the Salvation Army were wiped out of London, 'five thousand extra policemen could not fill its place in the repression of crime and disorder'.[41]

The Sacrament of the Good Samaritan

Although the Salvation Army is now principally regarded as a social welfare organisation, or at the very least a Christian body specially devoted to social work, Booth himself was very far from seeing it in that light. For him, the saving of souls was the only important issue: 'Alongside of this aspect of [a man's] condition, any temporal modification of his lot appeared trivial—nay, almost contemptible'.[42] He had abandoned his ministry in the Methodist church because the authorities wanted to make him spend time on parochial work while sinners were rushing headlong into the flames of Hell. He spoke of his work of salvation with the urgency of a man who was haunted by the spectre of damnation, compared with which any deprivation which might be felt in this life was utterly trivial.

Nevertheless, Booth recognised that those living in conditions of misery and vice would not be reached unless something could be done to change their circumstances. 'No one gets a blessing if they have cold feet, and nobody ever got saved while they had toothache',[43] was Booth's own rationale for becoming involving with welfare work. The poor needed to find a way out of their poverty, and, for those living lives which were actually vicious, it was even more vital to effect a complete change of lifestyle before the Christian vision could be attained. 'How can I be Christian—the life I'm living?', a prostitute asked at a revival meeting. 'You must give up that life', she was told,[44] but how? Women wishing to leave the only means of earning money which they knew needed help, both with accommodation and with job training.

It was perhaps inevitable, given the Army's commitment to working amongst the most desperate cases, that the needs of prostitutes wishing to change their lives should have constituted one of the earliest social causes to be taken up. Rescue work, as it was known, began informally, with Salvationists taking women they came across into their own homes. However, in 1883 a home was opened in Glasgow which put the work on a more formal basis. This venture appears not to have been a success, but in the following year a cottage was rented in Hanbury Street in East London for the same purpose. This time the work prospered, and the Army regards 1884 as the official beginning of its social work programme.

Taking on such a venture was a big risk for the Army at the time, with very little available by way of special funding, so it was imperative that the home became self-supporting as quickly as possible. The women were taught to cross-stitch the words 'Salvation Army' onto the regulation red pullovers which the soldiers wore, which raised 3s 6d per dozen, and they took in washing. This policy established one of the most important ground-rules for Army social work: that those receiving assistance should learn to pay their way in whole or in part as quickly as possible. Furthermore, those who had been helped were expected to help others in their turn. In 1891 an enormous tea party was held at the Crystal Palace for women who had been helped by the Army's social work programme, at which Mrs Bramwell Booth, the daughter-in-law of the General, launched the Out-of-Love Fund. Women who had been saved were asked to contribute one penny a week towards the cost of a new rescue home for 25 girls: 'Here is a beautiful chance for all saved rescue girls to repay, in some sense, the toil, the care, the love, and the expense which has been so freely and gladly expended on them'.[45]

In spite of the centenary celebrations in 1984 the Hanbury Street Rescue Home did not represent the Army's first venture in the field of social welfare. There had been soup kitchens in East London in the 1860s, and in the early years of the 1870s Booth had set up a series of Food-for-the-Million shops to provide cheap meals for the poor. These shops failed, partly because Booth insisted on appointing his son Bramwell, who was only sixteen, as manager. As a result, they are seldom mentioned in Salvationist histories, as Booth was a man who enjoyed talking about his successes, whilst ignoring the failures.

However, the experience of the soup kitchens and food shops was not wasted, because in January 1888 *The War Cry* announced 'A New Departure' for the Army: a hostel for the homeless on the West India Docks Road, Limehouse. According to Salvation Army tradition the inspiration for this work, for which the Army is still world-famous, came from a late-night journey which took General Booth across one of the bridges of London on a freezing night in the winter of 1887. He noticed men huddling in the niches of the bridge, with nothing but a newspaper to cover them. The next morning he told Bramwell to 'do something' about it: 'Get hold of a warehouse and warm it, and find something to cover them. But mind, Bramwell, no coddling'.[46]

The facilities which this warehouse offered, particularly by way of providing cheap meals, were very quickly put to the test during the dock strike of 1889. 'Had it not been for this place of relief the distress would have been much greater', said *The Times*, while, according to *The London Daily News*, 'it has been impossible to move about in the neighbourhood of the Docks lately without feeling one's self under a debt of obligation to them'.[47]

However, whilst charges were kept to a level which would be within the reach of all except the absolutely penniless, neither meals nor accommodation were given away free. Even during the dock strike, when the scale of hardship led to the rapid opening of additional shelters in former barracks at Whitechapel and Poplar, *The War Cry* was able to announce that: 'We have avoided, as usual, anything like mere charity doling but have offered all meals at half the usual price'.[48] Those who were penniless were given the chance to earn their keep in the labour shed or industrial workshop. Booth was clear about the objectives of his social programmes:

> I do not wish to have any hand in establishing a new centre of demoralisation. I do not want my customers to be pauperised by being treated to anything which they do not earn. To develop self-respect in the man, to make him feel that at last he has got his foot planted on the first rung of the ladder which leads upwards, is vitally important, and this cannot be done unless the bargain between him and me is strictly carried out. So much coffee, so much bread, so much shelter, so much warmth and light from me, but so much labour in return from him.[49]

This was a principle which ran through all branches of the Army's social work. The 'Mother' of a slum maternity hospital explained to a journalist in 1897 that: 'We don't *give* [clothes] away. We make them up in penny and two-penny bundles. People like to buy, and we like them to feel that they are not paupers receiving charity'.[50] Even an advertisement headed *Wanted! Young London Thieves*, which promised education and training for a better life, stipulated: 'Any thief is eligible. Entrance-fee 1d'.[51] All were expected to contribute towards the cost of their own salvation.

In Darkest England

The unshakeable public perception of the Salvation Army as a welfare organisation dates from the publication in 1890 of William Booth's book *In Darkest England and the Way Out*. He based his title on the recently published account of the explorer Stanley, *In Darkest Africa*, arguing that there were in England large numbers of people whose situation was just as horrifying as that of the natives of the African jungle. He called them the submerged tenth, the three million or so people whom he calculated to be living in poverty, misery and vice. Their degradation constituted 'the social question ... the greatest problem of our time',[52] and he intended to solve it.

Booth's blueprint for social regeneration, which came to be called the Darkest England Scheme, was vast in its extent. His plan involved a panoply of agencies to address every conceivable need, but it had three main constituent parts: the city colony, the farm colony and the overseas colony.

The city colony would take the homeless and the unemployed and get them back to work; the farm colony would train men in agricultural skills and fit them for work on the land, either in Britain or the colonies; the overseas colony would function together with the farm colony to give the trained workers a fresh start in another country. There were also plans for the reform of drunkards, prostitutes and criminals, for advice bureaux, legal aid and marriage bureaux, 'model villages', co-operative stores, holiday camps, refuges for street children and an agency to trace missing persons.

He costed the whole programme at £1 million, but said that he could make a start with capital of £100,000. The publication of *In Darkest England* was a sensational success, selling hundreds of thousands of copies in its first year, and raised discussion of 'the social question' to new heights. As a result, on 30 January 1991, only three months after publication, with contributions to the fund standing at £102,559, Booth signed the Darkest England Trust Deed, which established the social welfare work of the Salvation Army as a separate entity, with its own distinct funds—an arrangement which still pertains today.

The perception of the publication of *In Darkest England* as marking the beginning of Salvation Army social work is mistaken, as the Army had been developing social programmes of some sort since its earliest days as The Christian Mission in the 1860s, but there is no doubt that the book gave this social work both a higher profile and a greater degree of coherence. Many of the component parts of the Darkest England scheme had already been tried out by Booth before 1890, but that year seems to have been the critical one when key programmes were either developed or expanded.

One of the most important developments was the opening of the first 'elevator' in June of that year. It had become obvious, after the opening of the homeless shelters in 1888, that the only way to re-integrate the homeless into society was to get them back to work. Some had skills for which they had been unable to find purchasers; others were unskilled and needed training. To meet the needs of both groups the Army opened factories where they would be given the opportunity to get back to productive work.

Within the elevators a rigid class system was maintained, coupled with strict discipline. Newcomers were paid in two-penny tickets for their labour, four of which would secure bed and board. As their labour increased in value, so would the value of their tickets. Newcomers, or 'third class' men, slept in a first floor dormitory in wooden bunks with seaweed mattresses; 'second class' men slept in better-lit rooms on the floor above; while 'first class' men were given spring-mattresses, sheets and blankets. As the 1891 Review of the first year of the Darkest England scheme explained:

> All this visible, tangible reward of industry is part of the process of moral education which the majority of the ... inmates must undergo before they can be of much use to themselves or the world.[53]

By the end of 1894 there were seven elevators employing 1,000 men in tasks ranging from woodchopping and joinery to painting, tailoring and bakery.[54]

Moral Lunatics

Booth's book attracted an unfavourable notice from *The Times* because he complained that very little scientific research had been carried out on the causes of poverty. In a century which had been characterised by massive philanthropic efforts, coupled with intense critical discussion of the origins of 'the social problem' and the possible side-effects of charitable relief, this was an extraordinary claim to make. However, it reflected one of the less appealing sides of Booth's character, which was his unwillingness to acknowledge the work of anyone else in a field which he had chosen for his own.

No one was more identified with the critical scrutiny of charitable work than C.S. Loch, the Secretary of the Charity Organisation Society, which had been set up to co-ordinate the immense philanthropic efforts of the time. Loch promoted the doctrine, familiar to all those involved in the debate, of the distinction between the deserving and the undeserving poor.

This reflected a fear, which was shared by all the leading philanthropists, of 'pauperisation' or, as we would call it, welfare dependency. There was a particular concern that, if welfare efforts were concentrated in a particular area, like the East End of London, idlers would be attracted from elsewhere to take the handouts without any intention of trying to improve their own circumstances. The aim of maintaining the deserving/undeserving distinction was to concentrate assistance on those who had the will to become self-supporting.

However, Booth would hear of no such distinction since he regarded the social work as a means of securing the eternal salvation of those who were assisted, and he could not accept that anyone was 'undeserving' of salvation:

> The Scheme of Social Salvation is not worth discussion which is not as wide as the Scheme of Eternal Salvation set forth in the Gospel. The Glad Tidings must be to every creature, not merely to an elect few who are to be saved while the mass of their fellows are predestined to a temporal damnation ... As Christ came to call not the saints but sinners to repentance, so the New Message of Temporal Salvation, of salvation from pinching poverty, from rags and misery, must be offered to all. They may reject it, of course. But we who call ourselves by the name of Christ are not worthy to profess to be his disciples until we have set an open door before the least and worst of these who are now apparently imprisoned for life in a horrible dungeon of misery and despair.[55]

However, Booth's refusal to divide the poor into 'deserving' and 'undeserving' certainly did not mean that he was prepared to subsidise lifestyles characterised by laziness and vice. 'General Booth ... takes a very concrete view of the world as he finds it', reported *The Liverpool Daily Post* in 1890:

> Two things only he insists upon—first, that those who accept his aid shall be willing to work; and next, that they shall obey orders...His great rule all through is to be that, if a man will not work, neither shall he eat.[56]

Booth believed that even the lowest and most vicious should be offered the chance of a better life, and if they accepted and then failed, then the offer should be made again. However, for those who were so depraved as to resist repeated attempts to turn them away from vice and idleness, he recommended asylums for 'moral lunatics' where they would be prevented from going 'in and out among their fellows, carrying with them the contagion of moral leprosy'.[57]

Once it became clear that Booth's position was not so very different from that of the Charity Organisation Society, C.S. Loch revised his hostile opinion on the Darkest England scheme[58] and became an admirer of the General.

Darkest England and the Welfare State

Not all of the parts of the Darkest England scheme were destined to be realised, at least by the Salvation Army. Most of the institutions of the City Colony were already in place by the time the book was published, and the Farm Colony was established on 800 acres at Hadleigh in Essex in the following year, but the Overseas Colony, which Booth envisaged for Rhodesia, never materialised. However, it is a tribute to Booth's vision that almost all of his recommended agencies are now regarded as essential elements of welfare provision, like Citizen's Advice Bureaux, Legal Aid schemes and even recycling projects! Even the unrealised plan for 'Whitechapel-by-the Sea', to provide holidays for the poor, bears a striking resemblance to the holiday camps of today.

The ambitious scope of the Darkest England scheme has led Jenty Fairbank, the historian of the Army's social work, to describe it as 'a comprehensive ground plan ... which was to lead to the eventual establishment of Britain as a welfare state'.[59] However, Booth, whilst acknowledging that some people took the view that the state should be undertaking this sort of work, saw little chance of this happening in the foreseeable future, and in any case 'we are not quite sure if such an attempt would prove a success if it were made'.[60] He therefore believed that there was an immediate moral obligation on Christians to support his scheme, or produce something better. Furthermore, he insisted throughout the book (and, indeed, throughout his life) that the only way of helping the oppressed was to address their spiritual and moral needs, as well as the material ones:

> To get a man soundly saved it is not enough to put on him a pair of new breeches, to give him regular work, or even to give him a University education. These things are all outside a man, and if the inside remains unchanged you have wasted your labour ... All material help from without is useful only in so far as it develops moral strength within.[61]

> My only hope for the permanent deliverance of mankind from misery, either in this world or the next, is the regeneration or remaking of the individual by the power of the Holy Ghost through Jesus Christ. But in providing for the relief of temporal misery I reckon that I am only making it easy where it is now difficult, and possible where it is now all but impossible, for men and women to find their way to the Cross of our Lord Jesus Christ.[62]

In the Meantime

The purpose of the welfare work, as far as Booth was concerned, was the salvation of souls, but that did not make the material wants any less pressing. He was contemptuous of Christians who dismissed suffering by pointing to the glories of the life to come, or, as he put it, by 'drawing unnegotiable bills payable on the other side of the grave'. He was equally critical of the Socialist revolutionaries who were waiting for 'the general overturn' which would usher in Utopia:

> When the sky falls we shall catch larks. No doubt. But in the meantime? It is the meantime—that is the only time in which we have to work. It is in the meantime that the people must be fed, that their life's work must be done or left undone for ever.[63]

Nevertheless, as the years went by and the social work programmes of the Salvation Army assumed their tremendous dimensions,[64] Booth began to be tormented by doubts. Had it been a mistake to venture so far into the arena of social reform that the saving of souls—the only important work of the Army in his view—was taking second place? Would the Salvation Army become known as a social work organisation rather than a body to snatch sinners from the jaws of Hell? 'We were packed last night at the Social Lecture, and had a pretty good time, although I must say I am heartily tired of Social Schemes in places where I can get a crowd and get souls saved',[65] he wrote from one of his international speaking tours in 1902. When his son Bramwell tried to involve him in one of Josephine Butler's crusades he refused: 'My dear boy, I cannot go in for any more "campaigns" against evils. My hands and heart are full enough. And, moreover, these ... reformers of Society have no sympathy with the S.A. nor with Salvation from *worldliness* and *sin*. Our campaign is against *Sin*!'[66]

Whatever doubts Booth may have harboured about social programmes and campaigns of reform were futile by then. The social work had acquired a momentum of its own, establishing the Army in the public perception as the friend of the homeless, the destitute and the oppressed. This is an image it still retains, when most people know little of its religious work and absolutely nothing about its particular denominational stance. This was perhaps inevitable.[67] Booth himself was profoundly uninterested in theological disputes and kept the Salvationist creed to an absolute minimum of core Christian beliefs in the resurrection and the saving power of Christ's blood. He refused to introduce sacraments into the Army as he believed that any sacramental order provided a fertile field for disagreement, and he forbade Salvationists from making good this deficiency by receiving the sacraments in other churches. However, he urged his followers 'to observe continually the sacrament of the Good Samaritan'. They did and they still do, more than a century after the launch of his massive plan to enlighten Darkest England.

Free Spirits and Formal Structures

LOOKING back at the immense achievements of Christian philanthropy in the nineteenth century, one of the most striking aspects of
the whole culture was its reliance on the efforts of inspired and dedicated
individuals, rather than corporate bureaucracies. Because the *zeitgeist* of
our own time is so corporatist in hue, we tend to think that any large-scale
venture will have to be carried out by some statutory or official agency,
dependent either wholly or partially on public money. The Victorians
tended to take the opposite view. Not only did they *not* regard welfare
provision as coming within the remit of the state, they did not even see it
as necessarily the responsibility of the established churches. Christians
were expected to act in accordance with the dictates of their own con-
sciences, raising their own resources and operating at their own risk.

Of the three great Christian philanthropists whom we looked at in the
last chapter only Lord Shaftesbury was a life-long member of a mainstream church. He was a devout Anglican, deeply concerned for the
welfare of the established church and particularly for the evangelical
faction within it, but even he did not look to the official structures of the
Church of England to carry through the social programmes he advocated.

Barnardo and Booth effectively set up their own churches. Booth
abandoned his ministry in the Methodist church to establish what was to
become a worldwide Christian denomination, while Barnardo left the
Church of Ireland to join the Plymouth Brethren, but then drifted away
from them because he could not accept their absolute prohibition on
getting into debt. His impatience prevented him from waiting until the
money had come in before starting a new programme, and he preferred to
turn his visions into reality as quickly as possible, with the result that his
expenditures always outstripped his admittedly prodigious fundraising.
When he died in 1905 he left his organisation £250,000 in debt.

As we have already seen, his first great venture was the purchase and
conversion of The Edinburgh Castle from gin palace into a temperance
'coffee palace', with educational and leisure facilities for working people.
It was a grand scheme, impressively carried through. The Rector of Limehouse, the Rev S. Charlesworth, was invited to the opening and made a
complimentary speech which threw an interesting light on what people did
and did not expect of the church:

> I am utterly astonished at what had been accomplished. It is a most grand
> idea, a most sublime scheme. In the history of Christianity in England there

is hardly a fact to be compared with it—I had no hand in it ... The Established Church of England is not fitted for it; this work must be done outside of her; but I do feel the deepest reverence and admiration for those who have been engaged in it.[1]

Rev Charlesworth's testimonial was particularly generous in view of the fact that Barnardo had included within the Edinburgh Castle a mission church which he was to run himself, free from the doctrinal constraints of any one creed.

It would not be true, however, to say that the established churches did nothing, despite the impression which some of the philanthropists, and Booth in particular, tried to give. There were welfare organisations which were officially sponsored by the mainstream churches, many of which survive today. However, they were unable to rival the independent Christian bodies, either in terms of the resources they could command or in influencing the public discussion of social problems.

The Methodist Contribution

In 1868 a dynamic young Methodist minister called Thomas Bowman Stephenson took up his appointment as pastor of the Waterloo Road chapel in Lambeth. The area was impoverished and crime-ridden, and Stephenson could scarcely leave his manse without stepping over the evidence of the terrible neglect which children were suffering. He became convinced that he was being called to do something for them:

> Here were my poor little brothers and sisters sold to Hunger and the Devil. How could I be free of their blood if I did not try to save some of them? I began to feel that my time had come.[2]

In the following year, together with two Methodist Sunday School secretaries called Alfred Mager and Francis Horner, he opened a children's home in a converted stable in Church Street (now Exton Street), beside his church. A fund-raising pamphlet described its purpose as being 'to rescue children who, through the death or vice or extreme poverty of their parents, are in danger of falling into criminal ways'.[3]

The home became on official organisation of the Methodist church in 1871, and in the same year moved to larger premises in Bonner Road. Capable of receiving 100 children, the new premises opened in October with thirty seven boys and six girls in residence. A home was opened in Lancashire in 1872, and one of the first industrial schools for delinquent children opened in Gravesend in 1875. By 1900, when Stephenson retired as Director, the Home was caring for 1,150 children and was still growing rapidly. In 1908 the name was changed to National Children's Home and Orphanage, and in 1994 to NCH Action for Children.

Stephenson was one of the first to realise that children were not best cared for in large institutions, and he pioneered the cottage system, with a house-mother and house-father to 'surround them [the children] with all the influences of a Christian home'.[4] He also pioneered the training of staff and the development of an order of Sisters: trained, religious women who would be responsible for caring for the children. In all respects Stephenson was running neck and neck with Barnardo, who opened his first home in Stepney the year after Stephenson's Home in Lambeth opened its doors. It would be nice to say that they were in friendly rivalry, except that rivalries with Barnardo tended not to be friendly. However there is no record of any major falling out such as that which occurred between Barnardo and Edward Rudolf, who founded the Church of England Children's Society.

The Anglican Contribution

Edward Rudolf was a clerk in the civil service who also taught a Sunday School at St Ann's, Lambeth. One day he noticed that two of his pupils were missing, and he was distressed to find them later begging outside a gasworks. He learned that their father had died, and their mother had sent them onto the streets rather than let them go to the workhouse. Rudolf set about trying to get the boys accepted into institutional care, but found that only Barnardo's home in Stepney would accept them, as Barnardo made no other conditions than that the child should be in need.

Although Barnardo's was a fiercely Protestant institution, some Anglicans were concerned about the nature of the religious instruction which the children would receive there, as Barnardo was independent of any established church. Looking back on this incident later Rudolf recalled his concern that:

> ... after receiving definite Church teaching for some years, these little fellows should have to be placed where the religious instruction would be of a totally different kind, with the result that they would be lost to the Church of England.[5]

Rudolf managed to persuade Archbishop Tait, the Archbishop of Canterbury, that this was an intolerable situation, and in 1881 he set up the Church of England Central Home for Waifs and Strays. In 1946 the name was changed to The Church of England Children's Society and it is now known simply as the Children's Society.[6]

Barnardo initially welcomed the Society, saying that he did not 'care one fig'[7] about the denominational aspect of children's homes, as long as Christians were running them, but he changed his tone when he found that Rudolf's organisation was in direct competition with his own for funds. After a forceful expression of his views,[8] Barnardo responded to the challenge by setting up a separate fund within his own organisation for Church of England children. Ironically, Barnardo was later to become a member of the Church of England, although he kept very quiet about it, believing that it suited his purposes to be seen as an outsider.

Like the Methodist Homes, Rudolf's Waifs and Strays Society became involved in running industrial schools and reformatories, and began a long and fruitful ministry to handicapped children with the opening of its first residential home for physically disabled children in 1887. By 1900 the Society was running 80 homes and caring for 2,826 children.[9]

The Catholic Contribution

Welfare programmes instigated by the Catholic Church differ from those of other denominations in two important respects.

First, they tended to be modest in size and local, or diocesan, rather than national. The reasons for this were historical. For hundreds of years Catholics had been subject to persecution and discrimination, to a greater extent than any other denomination. During penal times the very act of celebrating Mass, which stands at the centre of Catholic life, was a criminal offence. The Catholic Emancipation Act had been passed in 1829, and the hierarchy had been restored in 1850, but the Church had not had time to develop the sort of centralised, bureaucratic structure which would have facilitated the formation of national Catholic charities. Welfare projects tended therefore to be 'one-offs', addressing a local need and often run by religious orders at the request of the local bishop. For example, Cardinal Wiseman invited the Sisters of the Faithful Virgin in Normandy to open an orphanage for Catholic girls in Norwood in 1848, and in 1860 the Sisters of Mercy opened an industrial school for girls in Brighton and Providence Row shelter for the homeless in the East End of London. 'Official' church sponsorship of welfare bodies was usually on a diocesan basis, with the result that there is no Catholic equivalent of Barnardo's or the Church of England Children's Society. There are still seventeen separate Catholic child welfare organisations, and although the Catholic Child Welfare Council was formed in 1929 to act as an umbrella body, initially comprising the diocesan societies of Westminster, Liverpool, Salford, Birmingham and Southwark, they continue to function separately.

The second important difference is that the Catholic welfare bodies were much more definitely sectarian. They were intended to benefit only Catholics and, in particular, to stop the 'leakage' of the faith which occurred when Catholic children were not given a Catholic upbringing. The Catholic child welfare bodies were formed for this specific purpose. It was not so much because there was no provision for destitute children available, but because such provision as there was would not enable Catholic children to grow up practising their faith.

The Catholic population of Britain was growing rapidly in the nineteenth century but much of it consisted of impoverished Irish immigrants, many fleeing the famine, whose children were likely to end up in the workhouse. Concern amongst Catholics over the 'leakage' of faith of workhouse children resulted in an Act of Parliament 1862, permitting the Guardians of the Poor Law to hand over Catholic children to Catholic schools and institutions and to make an allowance for their upkeep. This was strengthened by later legislation *requiring* them to do so.

Parish priests were encouraged to keep an eye on the Creed Registers in their local workhouses and to make application for the transfer of such children. This policy required the construction of the institutions necessary to receive them.

The history of the Southwark Catholic Children's Society can be taken as more or less typical. Bishop Butt of Southwark was worried that the Church was making no provision for the children whom the Poor Law Guardians were willing to hand over, and in 1887 he called a meeting at St George's Cathedral at which the Society was formed. It was originally called The Southwark Diocesan Education Council. In 1963 it became the Southwark Catholic Children's Society and in 1982, following the division of the diocese, it became The Catholic Children's Society (Arundel and Brighton, Portsmouth and Southwark).

The Bishop decided that a purpose built orphanage would meet needs more effectively than trying to convert individual houses, and so he embarked on the construction of an orphanage for 200 boys at Orpington, with a farm attached, even though he did not have the resources to pay for it. 'If we do the work God will find the money' was his philosophy.[10] An orphanage for girls followed. Other organisations, on a smaller scale, were run on behalf of the diocese by religious orders, like the infant school at Eltham, run by the Sisters of Mercy, and the home for severely handicapped children in Bexhill run by the Poor Sisters of Nazareth.

By 1897, ten years after its foundation, the Society was caring for over 1,100 children in six homes and schools for boys and twelve for girls.

Establishing Priorities

In one important respect there was no difference at all between the approach to philanthropy of the independent and the official Christian charities: they all believed that the relief of material deprivation was a trivial matter compared with the eternal salvation of the soul.

Unsurprisingly, perhaps, in view of their definite views on the conditions required for entry into a state of bliss, the Catholics were more blunt about it than other denominations. In his history of Fr Nugent, the founder of what is now the Nugent Care Society of the Archdiocese of Liverpool, Canon Bennett cited the example of two ragged schools run by religious orders in Liverpool:

Education was, of course, but a means towards moral uplift; and the primary object was to get these boys to Mass on Sundays. They were marched from the schools to the church by one of the Sisters of Charity, who were responsible for the school, and returned after Mass to the Ragged School for breakfast. What is touching about the story is that in order to secure their Sunday breakfast, though Mass was not until 10.00 am, many of these children would be at the school as early as 5 o'clock on the Sunday morning.[11]

It is easy to laugh at the idea of bribing boys to go to Mass with a hot breakfast, but this reflected the view that religious faith affects people's behaviour, and that the poor cannot be helped to escape from their deprivation unless they are addressed as creatures with a spiritual dimension. Canon Bennett was more specific about it later in his book. In discussing the vexed question of the high numbers of Catholics in the prison population, he argued that in Liverpool:

> ... of 5,281 Catholics committed in one year only sixteen men and four women attended Mass when outside prison, so their downfall was doubly assured. It is a matter of experience not sufficiently recognized by the general public that failure to practise their religion is at the root of the downfall of such Catholics as transgress.[12]

Perhaps the most forceful Catholic expression of this essential spiritual dimension to welfare work came from Cardinal Wiseman. In his *Appeal to the English People*, written in 1850, he spoke of the notorious slums of Westminster, 'nests of ignorance, vice, depravity and crime', but he made it clear that the problems were more than material. He described the slums as 'haunts of filth which no sewage committee can reach —dark corners, which no lighting board can brighten'.[13] It was these dark corners—the dark corners of the soul where evil intentions lurk—that Christian welfare programmes were uniquely qualified to illuminate. Otherwise, the Christian philanthropists would have said, what is the point?

Keeping the Faith

When Thomas Stephenson opened his first children's home in 1869 he sent out a fund-raising pamphlet which explained that the home was:

> ... commenced in humble dependence on the blessings of Almighty God, and it is hoped that its daily engagements will be pervaded by a religious spirit. For it is the firm faith of its founders that good citizens can only be found in good Christians, and that Christian philanthropy should aim at nothing less than the conversion of the soul from sin to God.[14]

Stephenson was able to rely on the support of a mainstream Christian denomination—the Methodists—to keep his work on track, but the situation of the independent Christian charities was more precarious. As is always the case with organisations started by dynamic individuals, the question looms, what will happen when the founder is gone? Will it remain true to his ideals?

Stephenson wrote an interesting review of Barnardo's work after his death, in which he praised Barnardo's great achievements, but expressed reservations about the future of the organisation. He felt that without the support of any denomination it might prove difficult to maintain the evangelical zeal which had driven it.[15]

Stephenson's concerns were to prove well-founded: Barnardos is no longer a specifically Christian organisation, and certainly does not see it as part of its role to evangelise (see pp. 75-76). However, the charitable bodies attached to mainstream churches have also faced challenges in maintaining their Christian identity, as we shall see in later chapters.

Philanthropy
and the Marketplace

The Great Principle of Self-help

LORD Shaftesbury, who must be ranked as one of the greatest philanthropists, disliked the term 'philanthropist' intensely and only used it
himself in a pejorative sense, in the same way that we would use 'do-
gooder'. He had such a fear of demoralising people with free handouts that
he regarded it as the method of last resort. In his opinion, as much as
possible should be achieved using the more character-forming methods of
self-help and the marketplace.

He expressed his admiration for the principles of self-help ventures
when he was laying the foundation stone of the Shaftesbury Park Estate
in Lavender Hill in 1872. The estate, a 'workmen's city' conceived as a
venture in mutual aid, was being built:

> ... on the very best principles ... the great principle of self-help, and the
> great principle of independence. By independence, I mean without any other
> assistance than that which every man has a right to receive from his fellow-
> man—sympathy and kind aid—and that is what every man, great or small,
> stands in need of from another.[1]

The Power of Self-interest

In addition to the principle of self-help there was also self-interest. If only
people could be shown that they could do good *and* make a profit, what
outpourings of philanthropy might it lead to! One of Shaftesbury's many
good causes was the Society for Improving the Condition of the Labouring
Classes, which built 'model dwellings' for workers which could be run at a
profit. There were never very many of these properties, but the intention
was to set an example to commercial landlords, showing them what could
be done. Shaftesbury involved himself with a project to build two model
lodging-houses, one in Bloomsbury and one near Drury Lane. In 1851 he
was proud to report that the Bloomsbury property was showing a return
of six and a half per cent.[2]

Few Christian philanthropists had a firmer grasp of commercial reality
than William Booth, and he gave the strongest proof of this with his match
factory. The sworn enemy of 'sweated' labour, Booth was particularly
appalled by the working conditions in the match manufactures. To keep
prices at rock bottom, manufacturers were producing matches dipped in

deadly yellow phosphorus. Working at close quarters with this caused necrosis of the bone, which became known as 'phossy jaw'. The bones of the worker's face would become infected, turning the whole side of the face green and then black, with fatal outcomes.

In 1891, just as he was launching his Darkest England scheme, Booth set up a Salvation Army match factory in East London where matches were produced tipped with harmless red phosphorus. The workers were paid 4d per gross rather than the industry standard 2½d, so the matches were that much more expensive. To publicise the work the Army would take tours of newsmen and MPs around the homes of matchworkers to show them the conditions under which matches were produced at 2½d per gross. At the climax of the tour the guide would extinguish the gas light to reveal an unfortunate woman glowing in the dark from the phosphorus which was eating her from within.

The matches, which with Booth's usual flair for public relations were called Lights in Darkest England, were extremely popular. The factory employed over a hundred workers and at its peak was turning out six million boxes a year. When the other match manufacturers realised that the public were prepared to pay more for a product made under humane conditions they stopped using the yellow phosphorus. In 1901 the managing director of Bryant and May told a Home Office committee that his firm had not used any yellow phosphorus for months. In 1908 an Act of Parliament was passed which rendered the use of yellow phosphorus in matches illegal, but the Act was almost superfluous as consumer pressure had already done the job.

The Merchant Princes of Philanthropy

Booth, Barnardo and Shaftesbury, together with many other philanthropists, were eager to use the market place as a means of raising funds for their projects, but they were not businessmen. There is another group of philanthropists who deserve to be considered separately, because of their peculiar circumstances: they were immensely successful businessmen who used their income to fund philanthropy on a scale which had never been seen before.

In his book *Enlightened Entrepreneurs* Ian Bradley examined the careers of ten giants of Victorian industrialism who shared the aim, expressed by Joseph Rowntree in the first issue of his *Cocoa Works Magazine*, of 'combining social progress with commercial success'.[3] These were men who created some of the greatest enterprises of the world's largest economy, and many of them are still household names. Bradley looked at Thomas Holloway (patent medicines), Titus Salt (textiles), Samuel Morley (hosiery), George Palmer (biscuits), Jeremiah Colman (mustard), Andrew Carnegie (steel), George Cadbury and Joseph Rowntree (chocolate), Jesse Boot (chemist) and William Lever (soap). He found two unifying features in their lives: their fervent adherence to political liberalism, in the nineteenth century understanding of that creed as represented by free trade and limited government, and their even more fervent religious faith, mostly of the Nonconformist variety.

Their support for liberal politics was the inevitable outcome of their own experiences as businessmen. It was the pursuit of limited government and low taxation, as expressed by such measures as the repeal of the Corn Laws and the abolition or reduction of taxes and duties on sugar, cocoa, soap and newsprint, which made possible the creation of a mass market in biscuits, chocolate, soap and other items which had previously been luxuries.

Their charitable activities were the outcome of their strict religious views on the responsibilities which attached themselves to the possession of great wealth. 'I hope we shan't lead an idle selfish existence,' Jeremiah Colman wrote to his fiancée, 'for I am sure that it won't be a happy one if we do. Influence, position and wealth are not given for nothing, and we must try and use them as we would wish at the last we had done'.[4] In spite of their great wealth these men lived modestly, often in houses within sight of their own factories. When George Cadbury was asked why he had such poor paintings in his house he answered: 'Why should I hang a fortune on my walls while there is so much misery in the world?'[5]

The enlightened entrepreneurs put just as much effort into giving their money away as they had put into earning it. They shared the views of other Christian philanthropists on the advantages of mutual aid and self-help and the dangers of 'pauperising' the recipients of aid by indiscriminate giving. Unsurprisingly, they placed a great emphasis on education as the most efficacious remedy against poverty. Jesse Boot paid for University College, Nottingham, now Nottingham University; Thomas Holloway created Holloway College in Egham, now part of the University of London; and Andrew Carnegie could be said to have founded the public library system with the 660 free libraries which he paid for throughout Britain.

However, the most interesting feature of the benefactions of these men is the fact that they were manufacturers before they were philanthropists. They could introduce, voluntarily, into their factories the sort of reforms for which philanthropists like Shaftesbury had to agitate in Parliament. Industrial nurses, doctors and welfare workers made their appearance, together with pension and life insurance schemes, and even schemes for worker participation.

Model Communities

However, some of them went much further. Six of the ten industrialists covered by Bradley's book moved their factories out of town centres onto what we would call green-field sites, convinced that the over-crowded and insanitary conditions of the inner city were having an adverse effect on their workers, both physically and morally. However, moving the factory was only the start of what turned out to be series of massive experiments on the old theme of the 'model' village or 'model' workers' dwellings. They built whole towns around their works: Saltaire outside Bradford, Bournville outside Birmingham, New Earswick outside York and Port Sunlight outside Liverpool.

This was philanthropy on a scale which had never before been witnessed. In the seventeenth or eighteenth centuries a wealthy merchant might endow a grammar school or a row of almshouses for a dozen worthy old people, and feel that he had made a major contribution to the welfare of the community. It took the profits of the Industrial Revolution to create townships for hundreds of families, living in houses which embodied the latest theories of health and sanitation, and supplied with parks, lakes, churches, schools, concert halls, educational institutes and swimming pools.

Titus Salt was the first to make the move, opening his magnificent new textile mill on the banks of the River Aire in 1853. Opposite the gates of the mill he built an equally magnificent Congregational Church, and from this axis of work and worship Saltaire spread out, covering 49 acres with 850 houses for 4,500 people. Salt paid to have the course of the Aire diverted to make the view more picturesque.

In 1879 the Cadbury brothers moved their chocolate factory from Bridge Street, in the heart of Birmingham, onto a 14 acre site to the south-west of the city which they called Bournville. Situated in open countryside, it became known as the factory in the garden. However the workers were still living in the back streets of Birmingham, so George Cadbury, who believed that 'no man ought to be compelled to live where a rose cannot grow',[6] acquired 120 acres of surrounding land in 1895 and began the construction of the village.

Bournville pioneered the concept of the garden city. The houses were built six to an acre and laid out so that it was possible to walk from one end of the estate to the other without leaving parkland. By 1901 there were 370 houses vested in the Bournville Village Trust, which Cadbury insisted must make a five per cent return on capital (which was reinvested in the village) in order to encourage others to set up similar schemes. Most importantly, however, Cadbury saw the material improvement in his workers' situation as the necessary condition for a moral improvement in their lives:

> How can [the working man] cultivate ideals when his home is a slum and his only possible place of recreation the public house? ... To win them to better ideals you must give them better conditions of life. The material and the spiritual react on each other.[7]

Cadbury's great rival, Joseph Rowntree, followed suit a few years later. In 1890 he bought 29 acres of land to the north-east of York and began moving his manufacturing operation away from the inner city five years later. In 1901 he bought a further 123 acres on which to build his rival to Bournville, the model village of New Earswick. He engaged Raymond Unwin, one of the pioneers of the garden city movement, as the architect and told him to design houses which would be 'artistic in appearance, sanitary, well-built, and yet within the means of men earning about 25 shillings a week'.[8] Like Bournville, New Earswick was put under the management of a trust. The Joseph Rowntree Village Trust was established in 1904 to manage the village and to promote experiments and reforms in housing management.

William Lever, whose soap empire owed much to the evangelical emphasis on cleanliness being next to godliness, also found his city centre factory inconvenient and unhealthy. In 1887 he bought 56 acres of land on the south side of the Mersey, called it Port Sunlight after one of his most famous brand names, and began production in a new factory there two years later. In 1888 he instructed an architect to begin drawing up plans for cottages, and by 1914 he had built 800 of them. Rather strangely, for a great industrialist, he was nostalgic for the 'good old days of hand labour'[9] and tried to create the sort of happy and harmonious community which he and others imagined to have existed in Merrie England. As well as providing canteens, swimming baths and a hospital Lever took great interest in his workers' cultural welfare. He built an art gallery as a memorial to his wife which he filled with a magnificent collection of paintings, and he engaged a musician to look after the musical life of the village. It was all, perhaps, too idyllic. As Bradley points out:

> For employees of Salts, Cadburys, Rowntrees and Lever Brothers the firm was a provider not just of wages but of housing, health care, education, recreation and entertainment. In the evenings there were company-run night schools and debates, at weekends company-run concerts and dances to attend and company-owned allotments to till, and on bank holidays works outings to the seaside or the country.[10]

Social Welfare as Social Control

The benefits which the enlightened entrepreneurs were able to confer on their employees were real and substantial: the mortality rates in Bournville and Port Sunlight were exactly half those pertaining in Birmingham and Liverpool. But it all came with a considerable measure of paternalistic control. Its most obvious manifestations were the minor ones: Saltaire, Bournville and New Earswick had no pubs. Titus Salt erected a sign at the entrance to Saltaire saying 'Abandon beer all ye who enter here', and he also banned smoking, gambling and swearing in the park. The more serious outcome of this admittedly benign tendency to arrange other people's lives for their own benefit was the effect it appears to have had on the political thinking of the philanthropists. Desiring that the whole population should have the advantages of the lifestyle which they had created for their own workers, they must have turned their minds to the question of what sort of organisation would be able to supply the good life on such a massive scale. They were already running some of the largest private corporations in the land. What could be bigger—except the government?

All of Bradley's ten entrepreneurs were supporters of the Liberal party, and five of them became Liberal MPs. However, in spite of the emphasis which Victorian Liberalism placed on small government and self-help, several of them belonged to what was called the radical wing of the Liberal party, which adopted a stance on some issues which was closer to socialism than to classical liberalism. Men like Cadbury, Rowntree and Lever saw a role for the state in the provision of welfare services and campaigned actively to secure it. Increasingly political action, rather than private philanthropy, came to be seen as the way forward. Inevitably, the attitude towards philanthropy itself began to change.

In 1901 Cadbury bought the *Daily News*, followed by the *Morning Leader* and the *Star*. He used the papers to campaign for minimum wage legislation, the nationalisation of the coal mines, more public works to reduce unemployment and an increase in old age pensions. Although he lost a great deal of money with his newspapers he did not regret it, explaining to his sons:

I had a profound conviction that money spent on charities was of infinitely less value than money spent in trying to arouse my fellow countrymen to the necessity of measures to ameliorate the condition of the poor.[11]

Joseph Rowntree shared his view. He condemned what he called 'the charity of emotion, the charity that takes the place of justice'[12] and called for a more radical approach:

I feel that much current philanthropic effort is directed to remedying the more superficial manifestations of social evils or distress, while little thought or effort is directed to search out the underlying causes of such evils or distress ... The soup kitchen in York never has difficulty in obtaining adequate financial support, but an enquiry into the extent and causes of poverty would enlist very little support.[13]

Rowntree had already set about remedying what seemed to him a glaring gap in the field of poverty relief by collecting statistics on poverty in York. His research was written up by his son Seebohm in his study *Poverty—A Study in Town Life* which was published in 1901, and which has come to be regarded as one of the seminal works of social science. More importantly, Rowntree set up the Joseph Rowntree Social Service Trust to fund social and political projects which would not normally be funded by a charitable body. His lavish endowment of the Trust has ensured that it remains the largest source of private funding for social policy research in the country. Its influence is immense, to the extent that the sort of projects favoured by the Joseph Rowntree Trust constitute the social policy agenda. Researchers who are unsympathetic to the Trust's left-of-centre viewpoint can find it difficult to obtain a platform for their work at all.

However, it was William Lever who, more than any of his fellow entrepreneurs, indicated the profound change which was coming over Christian philanthropy. In 1906 Lever became the Liberal MP for Birkenhead, and in the following year introduced a private members bill for state old age pensions, to be funded by higher taxation. His bill was taken over by the Government and passed in the following year as part of a package of measures associated with Lloyd George's so-called People's Budget.

As we shall see in the next chapter, the 1908 Pensions Act marked a watershed in welfare provision in this country. It was, in effect, a public admission that matters previously regarded as belonging within the province of self-help, family responsiblity or philanthropy had now been brought within the remit of the state. The fact that Lever, Rowntree and Cadbury supported state pensions showed how far the earlier evangelical view of limited state action had been modified. It is also quite probable that their own example of beneficent, paternalist provision of welfare benefits served as the inspiration for the creation of Britain's Welfare State. William Booth has often been credited with (or blamed for) drawing up the blueprint for it with his book *In Darkest England*. However, it seems far more likely that those architects of a welfare Utopia were influenced by the model communities of Bournville and Port Sunlight, with their happy workers joining choral societies and tending their allotments.

Priorities Reversed

It was not just the attitude towards welfare provision which had changed, but the that towards religion. William Lever was a Congregationalist, but his religious convictions were somewhat less passionate than those of the earlier evangelical philanthropists. After a trip to Egypt he complained that:

> The money spent on missionary effort is worse than wasted: the same money spent in taking little children out of the gutters in England, feeding, clothing and educating them decently until they are fifteen, then putting them in respectable service or the Colonies would do 10,000 times more good.[14]

This was a truly fundamental reversal of the position of men like Shaftesbury and Barnardo, who would have maintained that the salvation of souls was the most important thing, with material benefits coming a poor second. Lever's attitude was to become commonplace, but the downgrading of evangelical activity raises problems for the management of Christian philanthropy. If the spiritual element becomes subservient to the material element, then why should Christians become involved with welfare services at all? It might as well be left to secular bodies.

A Sea-Change

IN HIS magisterial historical survey *English Philanthropy 1660-1960* David Owen maintained that a fundamental change in outlook overtook philanthropic activity at the turn of the twentieth century.

For a period of about three hundred years, from the passage of the Elizabethan statute on charitable trusts in 1597, it was assumed that the provision of assistance to those unable to support themselves was primarily the responsibility of private citizens. The state was supposed to confine itself to political questions, principally the defence of the realm, and only to intervene in welfare as the supplier of last resort through the provisions of the Poor Law.

The history of philanthropic activity which Owen presents is a tribute to the magnificent achievements of men and women of goodwill who gladly shouldered this burden and, often against very trying odds, succeeded in the relief of suffering on a huge scale. However, towards the end of the nineteenth century the feeling began to grow that charity was not up to the task which it had been set and that at least some of its functions would have to pass to government. As Owen says:

> The balance did not shift abruptly or conclusively, nor was there a sudden and general acceptance of the notion of state responsibility for welfare. Yet the sky was full of portents, many of them as yet barely visible.[1]

Of at least equal significance to the feeling that charity could not cope with the burdens it had shouldered was the feeling that it *should not have to cope*, and that charitable activity was not an ornament but a reproach to a civilised society. As Gillian Wagner has shown, the death of Thomas Barnardo in 1905 provoked a certain amount of soul-searching on this score, including an article in the *Labour Leader* entitled 'Barnardo and Socialism' which argued that Barnardo's great work in saving 20,000 children (the real figure was nearly 60,000) was a shameful reflection on the state of the nation:

> Consider what amount of labour and money is spent upon public philanthropic schemes ... consider too if all these efforts were organised and economised into one whole national system for the prevention of destitution and degradation how great would be the result. Only by socialism can the nation do that.[2]

Charity and the state

To a limited extent there had been co-operation between the state and voluntary agencies dating back to the eighteenth century. During a brief and distressing period of its history, between 1756 and 1760, the Foundling Hospital had received funding from the government, as did the Royal National Lifeboat Institution between 1854 and 1869. Neither organisation wished to repeat the experiment.[3]

There had been a happier co-operation between the government and certain sections of the voluntary schools movement dating back to 1833, when the government began making annual grants to schools run by the National Society and the British and Foreign Schools Society. However, the grants never amounted to a large part of the schools' income, which was still mainly derived from parental contributions. The total subsidy was initially set at £25,000 per annum, compared with a voluntary expenditure on schools of £3 million per annum. As late as 1869, just before the Education Act which committed the government to the provision of elementary education, 'two-thirds of school expenditure was still coming from voluntary sources, especially from the parents, directly or indirectly'.[4] Many schools refused to accept grant aid at all as it entailed submitting to government inspection.[5]

The beginning of what we now call the contract culture, whereby the state pays fees to voluntary bodies to carry out duties which it would otherwise have to perform directly, can be traced to the reformatory and industrial schools, in which delinquent and neglected children would be cared for by charities who were re-imbursed for their expenses by the state. This arrangement was made explicit and formalised by the Youthful Offenders Act of 1854. The practice, noted above, of handing over Catholic children from the workhouse to be cared for by Catholic agencies, who were then re-imbursed by the Poor Law Guardians, also extended this principle of the transfer of public funds to charities.

These interventions were extremely limited, and neither the philanthropists nor the governments of the day wanted to see any substantial involvement of the state in welfare provision. Indeed, any such involvement would have been regarded by many as a threat to a free society. 'It is a principle of modern life in free countries', wrote Octavia Hill, the great housing reformer, 'that we are not directed from above, as a tool, but have to think out what is best to do, each in his own office'.[6] Lord Shaftesbury regarded what he termed 'State benevolence' as 'a melancholy system that tends to debase a large mass of the people to the condition of the nursery, where the children look to the father and the mother, and do nothing for themselves'.[7] The mistrust of big government was also a constant theme of Samuel Smiles who, in his great classic *Self-Help*, advised that:

> Prudence, frugality, and good management are excellent artists for mending bad times: they ... furnish a more effectual remedy for the evils of life than any Reform Bill that ever passed the Houses of Parliament.[8]

Political action, in his view, could never be a substitute for individual moral growth, although it might appear the easier option:

> It is ... generally felt to be a far easier thing to reform the Church and the State than to reform the least of our own bad habits; and in such matters it

is usually found more agreeable to our tastes, as it certainly is the common practice, to begin with our neighbours rather than with ourselves.[9]

Even the nineteenth century founders of the Christian Socialist Movement shared the general reluctance to invoke the powers of the state, particularly in what they regarded as essentially a moral sphere. As Brooke Foss Westcott pointed out, the law relies upon coercion, and therefore cannot 'work a moral revolution[10]... Good conditions of life, however needful for other reasons, do not make men good ... social improvement is bound up with individual improvement'.[11] Thomas Hughes, the author of *Tom Brown's Schooldays*, told a Co-operative Congress in 1872 that it was wrong to look to the state for the re-ordering of society: 'we have only asked the state to stand aside and give us breathing room and elbow room to do it for ourselves'.[12]

The Thin End of the Wedge

The first major assault on the view that philanthropy combined with mutual aid could deal with social problems, and that all that was required of the state was for it to 'stand aside', came with the Education Act of 1870, which committed the state to the provision of elementary education where no satisfactory charitable provision already existed. As we have noted above (see p. 25) the intention was not to destroy the voluntary schools, but to fill in the gaps in the existing network. In the event, the state quickly became more heavily involved than the supporters of the 1870 Act had anticipated, as the voluntary schools began to decline when the public realised that the government had accepted the ultimate responsibility for providing education. Many privately-run schools, including church schools, had to give up in the face of competition from the state, as the board schools, run by the local authorities, were able to use their state susbsidies to under-cut rivals' fees.[13] When the board schools abolished fees entirely in 1891 the effect on fee-charging charitable schools was even more serious.

However, the driving force for the creation of a welfare state came, not from any dissatisfaction with education, but from a growing feeling that the scale of poverty and unemployment, which seemed to afflict industrial societies on a cyclical basis, was beyond the scope of charitable solutions. In 1883 an alarming pamphlet entitled *The Bitter Cry of Outcast London* enjoyed a sensational success and focused discussion on what we would now call the underclass. Published anonymously, it had been written by a Congregational minister, Rev W.C. Preston, who believed that:

> ... without State interference nothing effectual can be accomplished upon any large scale ... The State must ... secure for the poorest the rights of citizenship ... the right to live as something better than the uncleanest of brute beasts. This must be done before the Christian Missionary can have much chance with them.[14]

The 1880s saw a severe economic depression which resulted in mass unemployment in industrial centres. There were attempts to raise charitable relief funds, like the various Mansion House appeals, but these were felt to have been inadequate and poorly administered. The question of the state's responsibility for the unemployed was being seriously canvassed.

However, discussion of the problem of poverty was made difficult by the absence of data. Alarming documents like *The Bitter Cry of Outcast London* (1883) and William Booth's book *In Darkest England* (1890) might stir the public conscience, but their claims could be dismissed by the unsympathetic as being exaggerated and based on subjective judgements. What was needed was a solid body of scientific evidence on the nature and prevalence of poverty.

The Statistics of Poverty

To resolve these uncertainties a Liverpool shipping magnate called Charles Booth (no relation to William) undertook the first major study of poverty to be conducted on scientific principles. Drawing on his own resources and working with only a few assistants, Booth published his massive seventeen-volume survey *Life and Labour of the People in London* between 1892 and 1901.

He came to the conclusion that, although East London had been chosen as the subject of the survey because of its notorious poverty, the proportion of the population who were actually in want represented a minority. He estimated that 13 per cent were very poor, and that only a small percentage of these would have been described by others or by themselves as being in distress. They included a small number of beggars, bullies, loafers and criminals (1.25 per cent) who degraded the working class with which they were associated. However, there was a larger class (11.5 per cent) who represented the real problem of poverty. They were ill-nourished and ragged, sometimes owing to physical or mental disabilities which made it impossible for them to be self-supporting, sometimes owing to drunkenness or fecklessness. Booth's view was that: 'It may with some reason be regarded as not so very bad that a tenth of the population should be reckoned very poor in a district so confessedly poverty-stricken as East London'.[15]

In spite of Booth's careful attempts to distinguish between the facts and the lurid pictures—painted on a curtain, as he put it—of poverty in London, the popular interpretation of his monumental study was that he had shown that *30 per cent* of the population were living in poverty. Like some of the famous and popular social science 'statistics' of our own time, the thirty per cent figure acquired a life of its own. People quoted it over and over again, without checking the source,[16] as if it were the clinching fact in the debate of charity vs. state provision. As David Owen put it: 'In the face of such a statistic as this ... the burden of proof would henceforth lie with those who continued to find in private philanthropy a satisfying solution to the social problem'.[17]

In spite of the fact that his estimate of poverty was more modest than that of some alarmists, Booth came to believe that the state would have to intervene in its relief. Was it not reasonable, he asked, 'for the State to nurse the helpless and incompetent as we in our own families nurse the old, the young, and the sick, and provide for those who are not competent to provide for themselves?'[18] He defended this extension of the role of the state by claiming that, if the state accepted responsibility for the lives of this small group of the helpless poor, it would help to keep it out of the lives of everyone else. As Owen said, 'this ... was to be a homeopathic preventive of socialism'.[19]

The State Pension

Booth also became convinced that poverty was 'essentially a trouble of old age'.[20] He consequently enlisted in the growing body of those who believed that the state should supply an old-age pension, unrelated to means-testing and therefore detached from the provisions of the Poor Law. This was a debate which had been gaining ground since the 1870s, when Canon Blackley took up the cause. Canon Barnett, the Warden of Toynbee Hall, included it as one of his measures for 'practical socialism' and, as we have seen in the last chapter, philanthropists like Cadbury, Rowntree and Lever supported it. The campaign was co-ordinated by evangelicals, with particular support from the Methodist and Congregational churches, and was based at the Browning Settlement in South London, the home of the Christian Labour Movement. They mixed prayer meetings with lobbying in what must rank as the first instance of a sustained campaign by the churches for a programme of state action in welfare.[21]

In 1891 Joseph Chamberlain became the first prominent politician to take it up, and the economist Alfred Marshall told a Royal Commission which had been set up in 1893 to study the question that 'extreme poverty ought to be regarded, not indeed as a crime, but as a thing so detrimental to the State that it ought not to be endured'.[22] He supported demands for a state old-age pension, but wanted a mechanism to discontinue the scheme once poverty had been eliminated!

Finally, in 1908 the Liberal government introduced the state pension to provide an income of 5 shillings a week to all over seventy whose income was below a given amount. It was estimated that it would cost over £10 million a year to administer, but the financial aspect of the scheme was not the critical one. Its symbolic significance lay in the way that it was based on an assumption that the mechanisms of self-help and philanthropy were not sufficient to deal with poverty. The state would henceforth have an ever-increasing role to play, which would in turn lead to a revision of the nature and scope of philanthropy.

By a strange co-incidence 1908 also saw the posthumous publication of B. Kirkman Gray's book *Philanthropy and the State*, of which, according to his widow, the original title had been *The Failure of Philanthropy*.[23] His

previous book, the first *History of English Philanthopy* (1905), had in
reality been more of a Fabian polemic than a work of history, and in the
sequel he expanded on his view of philanthropy, which was so negative as
to verge on the contemptuous. He regarded philanthropists as, at best,
misguided individuals stuggling against hopeless odds with tasks in which
they could never succeed. The only good thing he could find to say in
favour of philanthropy was that, by its very inadequacy, it forced into
public view social problems of such enormous dimensions that state
intervention became inevitable. 'The proper duty of the philanthropist is
to force society to do its duty.'[24] Gray attached great significance to the
campaign for state old-age pensions which was to result in legislation just
after his death ('the problem of the aged has been nationalised')[25] and to an
Act of 1906 under which the government undertook to provide school
dinners for the poor:

> The school dinner is an education in citizenship. Without a word being said,
> the child gradually absorbs a knowledge of its own dependence on and place
> in the social life. He finds himself a guest at the common table of the nation
> ... School dinners might be defended on the ground that they are unavoid-
> able, owing to the actual and unhappy circumstances of poverty. But when
> to this argument is added the assertion that such public provision is in itself
> a good thing, a fundamental change of opinion is clearly in process of taking
> place. If that claim is to be justified it can only be through the emergence of
> a new doctrine of society.[26]

He was right about the new doctrine of society. The twentieth century
would see a change from the view that welfare services are provided by
charity, with the state filling in the gaps, to the reverse assumption. Such
an intellectual revolution must inevitably have the most profound
implications for the social and economic order.

National Insurance

The 1908 Pensions Act was soon to be followed by legislation which had an
even more serious impact on the institutions of civil society. The 1911
National Insurance Act was intended to provide the whole working
population with the benefits already enjoyed by members of the friendly
and mutual aid societies. These societies allowed working people, including
some of the poorest, to insure against ill health and unemployment. They
were so popular that by the time of the 1911 Act there were already 6.6
million members of registered friendly societies, quite apart from those in
unregistered societies. Taking into account dependents who were also
covered by the policies, three-quarters of those covered by the 1911 Act—or
9.5 million out of 12 million—were already provided for. With membership
rising and coverage becoming ever more flexible, the mutual aid societies
could eventually have covered almost everyone.[27] However, the state
intruded with its regressive flat-rate tax which provided medical services
subsidised both by the employer and the government. Lloyd George

promised the workers 'ninepence for fourpence': they would contribute four pence per week, their employers would contribute three pence and the government two pence. The friendly societies were given a role as 'approved societies' but their character was radically altered by their enforced membership of the national insurance scheme, although they continued to be important until they were finally pushed aside in 1948.

The Post-war Welfare State

Jumping ahead, a raft of legislative measures in the years following the Second World War established the comprehensive, rights-based, cradle-to-grave welfare state which is now taken for granted. The National Health Service Act 1946 wiped out the voluntary hospital system, 'nationalising' 1,143 hospitals while at the same time seizing their endowments, 'the charitable trusts which witnessed to two centuries of concern for the sick and helpless'.[28] The Children Act 1948 gave the state primary responsibility for the welfare of neglected children; the Family Allowances Act 1946 subsidised families with more than one child; the National Assistance Act 1948 provided an income for the unemployed; and the Education Act 1944 had already enlarged the role of the state as principal provider of education.

The architects of the welfare state all professed their admiration for the voluntary principle, which they claimed (with varying degrees of truthfulness) to wish to preserve. In his book *Voluntary Action* Lord Beveridge called on the state to 'use where it can, without destroying their freedom and spirit, the voluntary agencies for social advance, born of social conscience and of philanthropy'.[29] In practice this new partnership, under which the voluntary sector became, in David Owen's memorable phrase, the junior partner in the welfare firm, has not been without its problems. Many charities found themselves bereft of purpose. In some cases they were offering to supply with voluntary contributions what the state was offering 'free', paid for out of tax revenues.[30] In others, like the Children Act, they found access to their client group obstructed by new statutory powers. Their freedom was curtailed as they were integrated into a system in which the state determined the level of services to which people were entitled as of right, and in which the very word 'charity' began to acquire the unpleasant connotations which still linger.

This partnership of welfare state and charitable bodies, which as early as 1934 was described and welcomed by one observer as 'the New Philanthropy',[31] has increasingly come to represent an arrangement for subcontracting. The attraction to the charities has been fairly obvious: by tapping into the resources of the Treasury, they have been able to increase their revenues to levels never before known in the voluntary sector. However there is an equally compelling, if perhaps less obvious, attraction to the government. Finding itself legally committed to providing a range of welfare services, the question arises, how are these to be delivered?

Even the most fervent believers in 'justice' of state provision of welfare have been confronted by the inescapable fact that state agencies are inefficient and expensive. Faced with ever-expanding demands for welfare, which are effectively infinite, but which have to be met within the framework of finite available resources, governments have increasingly resorted to a sub-contracting arrangement with charities as a means of saving money. The charities would provide the services for a modest fee—or, at least, less than it would cost to use government employees—so that the legal obligation was discharged at a reduced cost.[32] In other words, by enmeshing voluntary agencies in the state welfare system, the government found itself able to tap into their reservoirs of goodwill and volunteer helpers to provide a welfare state on the cheap.

This 'contract culture' of charity/state interdependence has now come to dominate the whole voluntary sector. The extent to which charities rely on sources of income other than voluntary donations by the public is made clear by the Charities Aid Foundation in its publication *Charity Trends*. The 1988 edition revealed that the top 200 fund-raising charities received only 57 per cent of their income from voluntary sources, with most of the remaining 43 per cent coming from local and national government[33]. Some smaller charities receive an even higher proportion of their income from non-voluntary sources: the charities ranking between 400-500 in the fund-raising league received 81 per cent of their income in this way.[34] As Frank Prochaska put it in his book *The Voluntary Impulse*, the state is now 'the largest single contributor to philanthropic causes'.[35]

The Threat to Voluntarism

From the beginning of the century, the threat posed to the voluntary sector by the growing presence of the state in welfare provision was a cause of concern to philanthropists. During the First World War the Rev R.J. Campbell, campaigning for the League of Mercy, used the Bismarckian welfare state as evidence of Germany's moral decline and warned that in Britain the state 'must never be allowed to supersede or absorb into itself individual responsibility and voluntary effort'.[36]

After the War the question of state funding for the voluntary hospitals became a topic of serious debate, as a result of the strain which the War had placed upon the whole hospital system. However, the Cave Committee on the Voluntary Hospitals in 1921 responded that:

> If the voluntary system is worth saving ... any proposals for continuous rate or State aid should be rejected.[37]

In the same year M.A. Spielman, a former Home Office inspector and a keen advocate of voluntarism in child care, warned that: 'the principle of voluntary management..is being seriously assailed'.[38] Spielman believed that the state was not equipped to act *in loco parentis* and that paid officials could not meet the needs of individual children. He was supported by William Hodson Smith, the principal of the National Children's Homes, who stated that 'people do not and will not give up their service to the State'.[39] Barnardo's, meanwhile, was struggling to remain true to the fiercely independent spirit of the founder and it worried members of its Council that the organisation was in danger of becoming 'the appendage of a Government Department'.[40] In its Annual Report of 1948 it assured supporters that it was 'an absolutely voluntary association, receiving no subsidy from the state'.[41] This was not strictly true, as it was receiving money from the Home Office for running Approved Schools, but it still derived over 90 per cent of its income from voluntary sources. This independence worried members of the Nathan Committee, which sat between 1950 and 1952 to consider reforming charity law, but, when they asked why Barnardo's was not pursuing state funding more vigorously, they were told that this was 'because our job is caring for children and not arguing finance with local authorities'.[42] However, both the National Children's Homes (now NCH Action for Children) and Barnardo's have overcome any initial reservations they may have felt about partnership with the state. NCH Action for Children curently derives 65 per cent of its income from fees and grants, almost all of which are paid by statutory authorities, and Barnardo's 42 per cent.

What Price 'Eternity Work'?

The question of the extent to which voluntary bodies are compromised by the 'contract culture', exchanging their independence for what is seen as easy money, is a large one, but the role of religious charities in this situation is peculiarly difficult.

As we have already seen, the founders of the great Christian welfare movements regarded the relief of material needs as almost a secondary issue: the important thing was the salvation of the individual's soul. If that required feeding the hungry, housing the homeless and finding employment for the unemployed, then all of those issues would be addressed, but they were means to an end. Georgina Battiscombe sums it up in her biography of the Earl of Shaftesbury (whom she refers to as Ashley in this passage):

> 'Are you zealous to redeem the time?' asked John Wesley. As Mr. Orchard remarks in his essay on *English Evangelical Eschatology*, that question was essentially an eschatological one. An eschatological awareness rather than a compassionate humanitarianism gave strength and urgency to Ashley's efforts on behalf of the poor, the oppressed and the outcast. The force which drove him was a passionate concern for souls. He believed that factory children, chimney-sweeps and lunatics all had souls to be saved and that very little time remained in which to save them. 'It is eternity work', said a Welsh Evangelical on his death-bed; men like Wilberforce and Ashley and, indeed, the Evangelicals as a whole, saw all social and charitable efforts as 'eternity work'.[43]

The question is, to what extent can tax revenues be used to fund eternity work? Is it realistic, in an increasingly secular society, to expect the departments of state to contribute towards saving souls? Will the acceptance of state funding by religious welfare organisations mean that they have to drop their evangelical and salvationist approach? And if so, why should they bother to continue with such work at all?

The Crisis in Evangelicalism

These are critical issues for Christians involved in welfare work and in the next chapter we will be looking at ways in which those organisations practising what William Booth called the sacrament of the Good Samaritan have adapted to life under a welfare state. However, another factor which must be considered in a history of church welfare work is the crisis in evangelicalism which occurred in the early part of the twentieth century.

As we have seen, the main dynamo which powered the engine of nineteenth-century philanthropy was evangelical Christianity. Other sects like the Jews and the Roman Catholics had their own welfare operations, but these were small in comparison and much more targeted on their own members. There was no Catholic equivalent of the Darkest England scheme, for example. It followed that any decline in evangelical faith or influence would have a profound effect on philanthropy.

This is, in fact, what happened. Theological liberalism had spread from Germany to Britain by the latter part of the nineteenth century. Coupled with other intellectual currents, of which Darwinism is perhaps the most famous, it presented a serious challenge to evangelicals, some of whom turned their backs on their evangelical upbringings, whilst remaining devout Christians. Evangelicals who remained constant to their theological position began to adopt an anti-intellectual and pietist stance and—most importantly from the point of view of philanthropy—to distance themselves from the world and its concerns, which were seen as irredeemably corrupt. This led to what has become known as the Great Reversal, which took place in the first two decades of the twentieth century. From being the leading figures in movements of social and political reform, evangelicals began to withdraw from such engagement in order to concentrate on the saving of individual souls, and the maintenance of orthodox, Bible-based teaching.[44] Following the deaths of Barnardo in 1905 and Booth in 1912, the line of great evangelical philanthropists was effectively at an end. Many of the organisations which these people founded survive, having coped in a variety of ways with the challenges posed by an increasingly de-Christianised society, but there were to be no more crusades on the scale of Darkest England.

As if this were not bad enough, the Christian philanthropies suffered further problems as a result of the widespread feelings of disillusion, resulting in many cases in loss of religious faith, which followed the First World War. Some of the subscribers to Christian charities began to look elsewhere for good causes. Charities with a scientific base, notably medical and hospital charities, profited to a certain extent from the difficulties which were being experienced by religious charities with more evangelical aims. From the early part of the twentieth century, therefore, it was clear that the spirit of the age would make life difficult for Christian organisations supplying welfare services.

What Future for Eternity Work?

Moral Welfare Scrutinised

IN 1958 the Church of England Moral Welfare Council commissioned a report into 'the scope and character of the work undertaken by the Church of England under the general heading of moral welfare work'.[1] The report, published in 1965 in book form, was an attempt to grapple with the question of whether or not the church should remain in moral welfare work at all, given the spread of state provision.

The authors admit that, although the scope of moral welfare work could be broad, it had in effect come down to providing services for unmarried mothers. Out of 130 homes listed in the Church of England Directory of Moral Welfare Work in 1961, 100 were being used for this purpose. However, by the time the report was commissioned there was also local authority provision for such cases, so the question arose as to whether it was worthwhile for the church to maintain a presence in the area at all. All the church homes received financial assistance from their local authorities, who were apparently happy to pay for women to stay there on the grounds that the church homes cost less than the local authority homes to run. However, some of the moral welfare workers interviewed felt that the church might just as well withdraw and leave it to the statutory authorities altogether, if they were no more than a cheap alternative to direct provision by the local authority.

The justification for the continued involvement of the church lay in its view of the moral dimension of human relationships:

> ... since man is made in the image of God, all human relationships in some sense exemplify His nature and purpose, but of none is this more true that the highest of all personal relationships, that between a man and a woman. Hence conduct that in any way degrades that relationship ... cannot be lightly regarded by the Church. Not only is such conduct socially deviant or inexpedient, it is sinful. But the very seriousness with which the church regards such behaviour lays upon its representatives a special responsibility for seeking out the sinner and offering not only social rehabilitation but newness of life.[2]

However, the extent to which any of the single mothers who were assisted were offered 'newness of life' appears to have been negligible. Although almost all the homes had a chapel and chaplain, with daily prayer services which the residents were expected to attend, the moral welfare workers themselves felt that the spiritual input they were able to make was almost nil. They claimed to have neither the training nor the time to address spiritual issues at all, with the result that the homes were providing little more than shelter and meals.

However, if the moral welfare workers thought they were doing too little by way of spiritual outreach, it is clear that some of the social workers thought they were doing too much. A questionnaire circulated to local authority officials elicited responses like: 'Moral welfare workers tend to form moral judgements of clients more than child care officers', and 'the very fact of working for a religious organisation suggests to a client "You have sinned"'.[3] The left-leaning research organisation, Political and Economic Planning, had already complained of moral welfare work in the following terms:

> There is a tendency to combine moral welfare work with compulsion to attend religious services, moralising and attempts at making converts for particular religions. Unmarried mothers should not have to pay the price of a pseudo-conversion for the help they receive, and from the point of view of the mother's resettlement such methods are not only objectionable but also ineffective.[4]

The General Secretary of the Moral Welfare Council denied the claims about compulsory attendance at services and attempts to make converts, but added that: 'there are religious and moral aspects of the problem and we should not be doing *our* job if we did not try to provide ways of meeting these particular needs'.[5]

The report is interesting because it provides a clear articulation of the problems that were arising for church welfare agencies as state provision grew. Many voluntary bodies have found themselves almost redundant as the state has taken over provision of the services they have traditionally offered. Some have attempted to carve out a new role for themselves as sub-contractors to the state welfare machine, but this raises new problems, the most serious of which is the loss of independence by the charities. Public money has to be accounted for, and it is inevitable that government agencies handing over payments to voluntary bodies to carry out certain services will want to control the nature of the programme. The scope for innovation— traditionally seen as one of the strengths of the voluntary sector—is therefore exchanged for what is seen as an easy source of funds.

For religious charities there is the additional problem that dependence upon a secular state welfare system may prevent the missionary or evangelical approach which was the original *raison d'être* of the organisation.

Paying the Piper

The threat which dependence upon government funds can pose to charities is well illustrated by the experience of the Mildmay Mission Hospital. It opened in the East End of London in 1892 as one of the Mildmay Institutions, inspired by the Rev William Pennefather, vicar of St Jude's,

Mildmay Park. Its aim was 'to preach the gospel and to heal the sick'. After functioning as an independent Christian charity for over half a century it was absorbed into the National Health Service in 1948. Funding would henceforth come from the government, although the hospital was to preserve its Christian character. However, by the early part of the 1980s the existence of the hospital was threatened by the policy of NHS rationalisation, which decreed that cottage hospitals of less than 200 beds were uneconomic. The Mildmay was therefore closed in 1982 'as part of a strategic review of all health services in Tower Hamlets'.[6] Absorption into the state sector had proved to be a mixed blessing.

A campaign was launched to revive the Mildmay as an independent Christian voluntary hospital, operating outside the NHS. However, without having apparently learned their lesson, the campaigners still thought in terms of getting the money from public sources, principally the Regional Health Authority and the Department of Health. The property was returned to the League of Friends on a 99-year lease at a peppercorn rent and it re-opened in October 1985. The intention was to care for the chronically ill, the disabled and the very frail, but everything still depended on the sort of projects which public health professionals were prepared to finance.

The re-born Mildmay Hospital was coming on-line at the time when the AIDS lobby was assuming its pre-eminent position amongst the special interest groups demanding public funds. As the stopcocks opened and AIDS funding began to flow it soon became apparent that the money which was being made available was out of all proportion to the numbers affected.[7] Furthermore, AIDS funding was 'ring-fenced', and hospitals soon learned that the easiest way to obtain grants for research or healthcare was to make sure that every proposal carried an AIDS component.

From 1987, when the Mildmay converted one of its three wards for the care of AIDS patients, its income seemed assured. The government contributed £200,000, and further donations of £280,000 had been received by the beginning of 1988. As for the other patients, including the young chronically sick, 'it was more difficult to attract interest in, and raise funds for, those patients than for AIDS'.[8] Perhaps inevitably, treatment for these patients came to an end and the Mildmay was turned over exclusively to AIDS. Given the continued dependence on public sources of funds, it is unlikely that any other course of action was possible. The accounts for 1994 show that nearly 70 per cent on the Hospital's income came from agencies of the state. Instead of pursuing their original vision, the Hospital's board had ended up following the dictates of fashion in health-care funding.

The Mayflower Centre
The history of the Mayflower Family Centre in Canning Town illustrates even more clearly the double-edged nature of state funding for charities.

The Centre was founded in 1894 as the Malvern College Mission, inspired by the university settlement movement of the time, of which the most famous example was Toynbee Hall. The purpose of the settlements was to bring together rich and poor by involving privileged young men and women from public schools and universities in an ongoing commitment to welfare projects in poor areas. The missioner described the aim in *The Old Malvernian* as '... to carry on the church's work amongst her people from both a religious and social point of view and to be a centre of religious influence and social good'.[9]

One of the Mission's earliest wardens was a larger-than-life character called Reginald Kennedy Cox, who insisted that what people in deprived areas needed was beauty. He transformed the ramshackle collection of cottages and sheds into a half-timbered court, resembling an Oxbridge College, with a chapel based on the Great Hall of Lincoln's Inn and a theatre for the performance of Shakespeare and opera, with 'modern problem plays strongly excluded'.[10] He instituted clubs for young people and for adults, a Saturday night film show to provide an alternative recreation to the pub, and a Sunday cycling club to provide outings for young people to country locations, where tea and a religious service would be provided by the vicar. All social work, in his view, had to have a religious basis. There were several football teams in Canning Town which had no access to a pitch. Kennedy Cox agreed to provide the pitch on condition that the men attended a short Football Service before each game.

Kennedy Cox was well connected socially and funds for the various activities in the East End were raised at lavish functions held in the West End. There was a jumble sale which lasted for two days, and an Empire Ball and Pageant for which he booked the Albert Hall for a week. He renamed the Mission the Docklands Settlement and, as other similar ventures were set up in imitation, Canning Town became Docklands Settlement No. 1 in the Docklands Settlement movement.

By the 1950s it was felt by some that the Settlement had outlived its usefulness. The social needs of the area were very different and, with the advent of a welfare state, the role of the church in meeting them was no longer so clear. In 1956 it was decided to close the Settlement and sell the site for development. Malvern College also decided to withdraw from its involvement in the area. However a committee, put together by the Bishop of Barking and Rev David Sheppard, took over the running of the Settlement and in 1957 its name was changed to Dockland Family Centre, with David Sheppard as Warden. It was incorporated as the Mayflower Family Centre in 1958.

Under David Sheppard the emphasis on youth work, which had characterised the Centre since its inception, continued. The ultimate aim was for the venture to become a local initiative, no longer dependent on outside help, and to this end resources were channelled into reaching young people who could be given the confidence to become local leaders. A

Housing Association was formed to encourage young families to stay in the area and assist with its development rather than moving 'up-market' and out as soon as they were able.

David Sheppard was a charismatic figure and a national celebrity before he came to Docklands, and during his years as warden the Centre enjoyed a high public profile and generous support. When he departed to become Bishop of Woolwich there was a drop in donations and, some sensed, a loss of direction. In 1974, at the instigation of a new warden, it was decided to launch a major redevelopment of the whole site, with a new youth club, sports hall, training centre, day centre for the elderly and other facilities. The working party of nine people contained only two local church members, and it was obvious that a project on this scale could not be handled by a small congregation in a poor area. As one of the church members said, if outsiders wanted to come in and build a new centre, they could, but they should not expect the local people to run it. Another complained that the efforts which had been going into building up a local community were now being directed into bricks and mortar.[11]

The re-development cost £1 million, and that was after some of the more expensive elements had been dropped. Half of this came from public bodies, with the Sports Council paying for the sports hall and Newham Borough Council assuming responsibility for most of the salaries of the youth workers and the manager of the sports hall, as well as a substantial community-work grant. The heavy dependence on the Council soon brought to the fore the tensions which often arise when charities, and particularly religious charities, look to public funds rather than voluntary giving for support.

The first danger signal was related to the nursery school, which had been a long-established part of the Centre's activities. It was losing money and Newham Council was prepared to take it on, but the Mayflower Council asked for majority representation on the board of management in order to ensure that it would continue as a Christian school. This was refused, together with a further request that the continuation of religious education should form part of the agreement. The school now functions independently of the Centre and is not a Christian school.

The second warning sign arose from the appointment of a manager for the new sports hall who was not a Christian. As a result of friction he resigned soon afterwards, and a decision was taken that senior staff should be Christians. In his history of the Mayflower, *A Different Kind of Church*, Peter Watherston makes a comment on this which is significant in view of the problems which have been experienced by a number of Christian charities in retaining their identities as they become absorbed into a state system:

> In an eagerness to meet the ongoing needs of the area or get a particular project off the ground, there is always a temptation to go for what seems to produce the greatest practical benefit. This often involves appointing people

with enthusiasm and expertise but with little if any Christian conviction. It is justified on the grounds that they will be influenced towards Christianity by the rest of the team. Usually the reverse is the case. Many Christian organizations have done this and have moved away from a biblically-based mission so that in the end the Christian content is reduced to a general desire to do good to others.[12]

In 1982 Edward Furness and Peter Watherston were appointed warden and chaplain of the Mayflower Centre. They found themselves in charge of what was, in effect, a medium-sized social work organisation with a small church attached, and not a great deal of connection between the two. Furthermore, the youth work did not always seem to embody the basic Christian belief that lives can be changed and mended by faith. Edward Furness asked:

> Was it too heavy to speak of the burden of sin to people who were often put down and made to feel inadequate? Should I look for conversions, for lives changed by Jesus, or was I to stay alongside the hurting people for ever? And what about the Holy Spirit about whom there seemed to be a respectful silence?[13]

Edward Furness and Peter Watherston wanted to re-create the whole operation by going back to basic principles. This was at a time when Newham Council was becoming increasingly occupied by multi-culturalism, equal rights and gender issues. The Council became more demanding about what was expected from recipients of grant aid and the Centre's evangelistic outreach caused resentment.

The Crisis with the Council

Things came to a head in 1989 when the Borough Council wanted to take over the running of the youth club building, which was not being used at the time. Although they were tempted by the offer of £10,000 a year, the Mayflower Council turned it down on the grounds that some of the uses to which the Council might put the building could conflict with the Centre's Christian foundation.

The Council's officers responded by stating that a condition of grant aid was the ability of organisations to comply with the Council's equal opportunities policy. Edward Furness and another Mayflower Council member were summoned to a meeting at which they were asked if the Mayflower Centre would be made available to Muslims teaching the Koran or to lesbians promoting their lifestyles. They answered no to both questions, as lesbianism and the worship of other gods are contrary to Scripture. Both situations were hypothetical: there had been no problems about making facilities available to outside groups.

The Council announced that the Mayflower Centre would be monitored for six months with a view to terminating all grant aid. Meanwhile council members were advised not to use it for meetings or attend meetings there. This reduced income from lettings as groups which needed councillors to attend their meetings were nervous of holding them at the Mayflower.

As a result of lobbying by local people and mediation by the Bishop of Barking an equal opportunities statement was agreed with the Council and funding continued. However, one year later all grant aid from the Council was cut off. Peter Watherston did not regard this as an unqualified misfortune. He wrote in the July 1991 edition of *Mayflower News*:

> ... in recent years there has been an increasingly narrow focus on work eligible for grant aid and an increasingly strong control from the local council in what is done and how it is done. There is a real danger that voluntary organizations receiving grant aid will become puppets of the authority. Though we face an uncertain future we value having the freedom to move in the way we believe God is directing and to trust Him for the resources needed to get there.[14]

In each of the years since the withdrawal of the Council grant (which has since been followed by the withdrawal of financial support from the Anglican diocese) the accounts have shown a small surplus, and there has been no reduction in services. On the contrary, hostel accommodation has been added for those who need supervised or assisted accommodation at a cost of £250,000, with no public money or even a general appeal being required. In the financial year ending March 1994 the total income of £188,000 was all either self-generated or the result of voluntary giving, apart from approximately £20,000 received in housing benefit for the residents of the hostels.

Faith in the Government

Then and Now

CHAPTER 3 reviewed the work of three of the greatest Christian philanthropists: Lord Shaftesbury, Thomas Barnardo and William Booth, all of whom founded organisations which are still functioning today. An examination of the way in which they now operate should reveal something about the changing role of the voluntary sector in a welfare state.

The most obvious difference which their founders would notice, were they to return today, is the dependence upon public money rather than voluntary giving.

The Taxpayer as Philanthropist

The accounts of the Social Work Funds of the Salvation Army (which have to be kept separate from the Central Funds for religious work) show an income in the year 1993/4 of just over £12 million. This comprises voluntary giving—donations and legacies—as well as self-generated income from investments and property. However, the expenditure columns show, as deductions from the costs of running the social work programmes, very considerable sums of additional income.

The total cost of running the social work programmes for the year came to just over £34 million, of which 75 per cent was recouped from income associated with them. Some of the items represent self-generated income, like fees paid by people who are using the Army to trace missing relatives. However, the bulk of these large sums comes from public bodies. There are some direct grants from local authorities towards the cost of homes and centres, but most of the money comes in the form of payments for food and accommodation. The elderly residents of the Army's old people's homes are paid for under contract by the local authority, while the residents of the hostels for the homeless are required to pay a nightly fee for bed and board. Sometimes these payments are made in the form of direct transfers from the welfare departments direct to the Army, but some local authorities refuse to do this and insist that the homeless apply in person for their housing benefit, which they receive in cash. It is then up to them to make the payment to the hostel. In some cases the homeless may have earned the money themselves or come by it in other ways such as begging. The Army takes the view that, if it makes a charge for services, it is not up to its officers to quiz people as to how they came by the money. It is not possible, therefore, to make exact calculations, but it can be said with confidence that a large part of the Army's social work programme is, in fact, funded from public money, either directly or indirectly.

Barnardos is in a more direct contractual relationship with the welfare state, since it obviously cannot charge the children for their own care. Out of its 1993/4 income of nearly £73 million, over £33 million, or 46 per cent of the total, came in the form of fees and grants from public bodies.

The Shaftesbury Society, which is the old Ragged Schools Union so beloved of the Earl, is the most heavily dependent on public funds. Over 80 per cent of its income of just under £20 million in 1994/5 came from public funds. According to the Society's Chief Executive: 'we expect local authorities to pay for assessed client services without calling upon charitable resources which should be reserved for capital spending'.[1]

Perhaps the more serious question is, to what extent does dependence upon public funding compromise the ability of Christian charities to imbue their work with the moral and spiritual dimension which is the distinguishing characteristic of faith-based welfare work? In the last chapter we saw how conflict developed between the Mayflower Centre in Canning Town and Newham Borough Council over this question. However, the Mayflower is a small organisation which could not expect to exert much influence over public policy. The situation should be different for the major players: Barnardos is the largest childcare organisation in the country, and the Salvation Army is the largest supplier of welfare services after the government. These organisations should be in a position to influence the framework of public policy within which they operate.

The Salvation Army

This is certainly the case for the Salvation Army. In 1989 the Army sponsored a major research project into the nature and extent of homelessness in London. The results of the numerical count established that there were approximately 75,000 homeless people in London of whom about 2,000 slept 'rough' in the streets each night. These figures contributed to the launch of the government's Rough Sleepers Initiative in 1989 with a budget of £96 million. Among the specific proposals was the setting up of temporary night shelters for the winter months, offering homeless people bed and breakfast accommodation only. However, the Army was only prepared to participate in the Initiative on its own terms, providing full-time care and accomodation with three meals a day. Residents of the Army shelters were encouraged to become involved in a resettlement programme to prevent them from having to go back on the streets when the Rough Sleepers' Initiative came to an end. The Army's approach was so successful that, after an initial review, the government would only offer funding to organisations working on the same basis.

The Salvation Army remains an overtly Christian organisation. According to its annual report for 1992/3:

> We are a branch of the Christian church, and our officers are recognised ministers of the gospel ... our religious activity is permeated by a robust

social concern. And our social work is motivated by a vibrant spirit of Christian caring.

The religious aspect of its social work programme has exposed the Army to criticism. A television documentary entitled *For God's Sake Care*, broadcast in 1981, included, amongst other criticisms of the Army's work for the homeless, the charge that residents in the hostels were being pressurised into attending religious services, even though attendance was optional. This was clearly regarded by the programme's makers as taking unfair advantage of the poor. The response from the General of the Army, Arnold Brown, showed how closely the Army had adhered to the Founder's vision:

> The Salvation Army is a movement for Christian evangelism taking the Gospel to the unchurched. It is not concerned only with the provision of food, clothing or shelter, but with the totality of human need ... Our aim is not simply to ameliorate but to assist divine grace in changing the life-style and raising the hopes of the downtrodden and dispossessed.[2]

The Army maintains William Booth's position that material assistance can only be effective when it is part of a holistic concern for the moral and spiritual condition of the person being helped. For this reason the Army holds daily prayers in each of its centres, although attendance is always optional. The chaplain to the Army's social work sits on its most senior policy making committees, there are spiritual retreats for officers and employees and a spiritual campaign for one week every November.

The Shaftesbury Society

The Shaftesbury Society is also an overtly religious body. Its chairman is a clergyman who writes in the Annual Report for 1994/5 that:

> We set out to achieve God's purpose by showing the love of Christ in all we do—by caring for others, not because we have to...but because we want to.

He goes on to express the hope that 'God has provided in the past and we look to Him to provide for all our needs in the future'. Unfortunately, as the Society has allowed itself to become dependent for almost all of its income on public bodies, God has to make this provision via the finance committees of local authorities, and they seem reluctant to oblige. The same report contains the announcement that 'the Society has concluded that we can no longer support those urban churches and missions who cannot be self-financing'.

Barnardos

Barnardos has undergone a more fundamental change in its recent history than the other bodies. Traditionally Barnardos described itself as Christian-based. Applicants for jobs were asked at the interview stage if they were in sympathy with this Christian basis, and those in senior positions were expected to establish a fuller accord with the organisation's Christian foundation. However, by 1990 it was felt that the work of

Barnardos was increasingly with those of other faiths and none, and that the Christian bias had become a stumbling block. In 1991, after a major consultation process, a statement of Basis Values was issued which described Barnardos as:

> ... an association whose inspiration and values derive from the Christian faith. These values, enriched and shared by many people of other faiths and philosophies, provide the basis of our work ...
>
> ... In a multi-cultural society we continue to recognise and respect our Christian foundation while embracing the changing circumstances in which we live ... Barnardos welcomes staff and volunteers from all world faiths and philosophies and the diversity they bring.

As well as the commitment to multi-culturalism, there are aspects of the ways in which the charity now operates which would surprise its founder. A series of television programmes on the work of Barnardos, broadcast in 1995, showed two project workers approaching teenage boys who were working as prostitutes in London's West End. Amongst other things, they were providing the boys with condoms, and explaining the differences between the types used for oral and anal sex. Although members of staff interviewed for the programme expressed the view that, if Barnardo were to return today, he would approve of the modern methods, it seems highly questionable that he would have regarded providing sexually exploited teenagers with condoms as a suitable response to their needs.

However, Roger Singleton, the present Senior Director of Barnardos, is emphatic that changes in the organisation do not reflect pressure from statutory funders, and that the decision to review the Christian basis was taken within the organisation.[3]

The Small Print of Contract Culture

Charities operating in the contract culture enjoy levels of resources undreamt of by their founders, with budgets running into eight figures. However there has been, for some at least, a price to be paid in terms of maintaining their original identity.

As the organisations have expanded they have acquired large staffs, most of whom enter via the social work sector rather than through church channels. Often those adhering to the original spiritual vision of the founder find themselves outnumbered by those who have no particular religious beliefs, or at least no essentially religious view of social welfare work. This can lead to head-on conflicts, as occurred in the Children's Society in 1994 when several members of staff resigned after a bitter battle with the governing body to establish a policy of placing children with 'gay carers'. The Council took the view that, as a Christian organisation closely linked to the Church of England, they should support marriage as the social context most suited to the upbringing of children. Although some staff objected that they were failing to meet the requirements of the Children Act, which bans discrimination against particular groups, the Society claimed that as a voluntary organisation it was not obliged to offer a comprehensive service, and could refer children who requested 'gay carers' to other organisations. One of the members of staff who resigned claimed that he had never known this to happen.[4]

Welfare Dependency

In the case of some Christian charities there has been a move away from the idea that those assisted should be speedily enabled to get back on their own feet. This was one of the articles of faith of nineteenth-century philanthropists who regarded pauperisation (or welfare dependency, as we would call it) as a terrible thing to be avoided by charities at all costs. When disputes arose between philanthropists it was often over this question, with rivals accusing each other of encouraging dependency. C.S. Loch, the Secretary of the Charity Organisation Society and the sworn enemy of indiscriminate giving, originally criticised William Booth's welfare work with the Salvation Army on the grounds that he would not weed out the deserving from the undeserving poor, but Booth himself was just as conscious of the dangers of 'pauperisation', and wrote:

> We are not opposed to charity as such, but to the mode of its administration, which, instead of permanently relieving, only demoralises and plunges the recipients lower in the mire, and so defeats it own purpose.[5]

William Booth believed that Christian conversion and self-help went hand in hand since Christianity, at least in its evangelical manifestation, encouraged virtues which could not but make a man upright and productive, such as honesty, industry, sobriety and self-respect. As an article in one of the Army's periodicals put it: 'the tendency of all saved people is to gravitate upwards and not downwards'.[6]

Modern Christian charities, on the other hand, in at least some cases, seem to regard life on welfare as a valid option, and even offer training for it. Projects for the homeless tend to be based on the assumption that the ideal solution is to get the sufferer onto the right combination of welfare benefits. Whereas William Booth used to boast of the numbers of homeless men he had been able to get off the booze, on their feet, re-united with their families and back into the workforce, the annual reports of some modern charities for the homeless, including the Christian-based ones, are more likely to detail the numbers who have been helped into council flats and onto income support.

However, it would be unreasonable to blame the charities for taking a view of welfare provision which is widespread throughout society. When the British Social Attitudes survey asked people if they thought that government or charity should be responsible for the provision of selected welfare benefits, a large majority thought that the government should be either entirely or mainly responsible. In the case of housing for the homeless the figure was 82 per cent.[7]

Nevertheless, when Christian welfare organisations begin to act as funnels for the welfare state, bringing more and more people onto the long list of DSS beneficiaries, we have to ask what view of human nature they take, and what they regard as the ultimate determinants of human behaviour.

Deserving and Undeserving Poor

It all depends on what you see as the cause of poverty. The hard-line, Victorian evangelical view, which was crystallised in the approach of people like C.S. Loch, Octavia Hill and the other leading lights of the Charity Organisation Society, was that large numbers of the poor were responsible for their own plight, which resulted from moral failings such as drinking, idleness or dishonesty.[8] As Samuel Smiles put in *Self-Help*:

> What we are accustomed to decry as great social evils, will, for the most part, be found to be but the outgrowth of man's own perverted life.[9]

In order to assist, charitable organisations were urged to divide the poor into deserving and undeserving. The deserving poor were those who could be helped by short-term financial assistance or by moral guidance or both. It was here that the influence of religious belief was so important. By offering the chance of moral and spiritual renewal the religious philanthropist could refresh those parts which a state-run system could never reach. People were not excluded from assistance just because they had moral failings, but they had to show at least a willingness to reform. The undeserving poor, on the other hand, were those who had sunk into such moral degeneration that there was neither desire nor intention to reform. They could only be left to the Poor Law. Many philanthropists made this their line of demarcation between the spheres of charitable and state action, leaving the state to deal with individuals who showed no willingness whatever to reform themselves.

Such an attitude towards the undeserving poor now seems harsh, and would find few modern supporters. However there has been a move to the opposite extreme. The idea that most people are responsible for their own poverty has been replaced by the belief that nobody is. In the view of many professional welfare lobbyists, the poor and the suffering are scarcely to be regarded as moral agents at all, or even mentally competent. Things just happen to them. It must all be the fault of the system, or the government, or the environment.

Habits or Habitations?

The nub of the problem was put by Samuel Morley MP, hosiery tycoon and mega-philanthropist, in the middle of the nineteenth century:

> Many people begin at the wrong end. They say people drink because they live in bad dwellings; I say they live in bad dwellings because they drink. It makes all the difference the way you put it. The first essential is not to deal with the habitation, but the habit.[10]

There are numerous examples in the charitable sector today of dealing with the habitation first.

The Passage, in Victoria, is London's largest day centre in London for the care of the homeless. It is run by the Daughters of Charity with the backing of Westminster Cathedral, the Roman Catholic community and many other churches, organisations and individuals, particularly in the London area. It does a great deal of good work, and there is little doubt that homelessness would be a more serious problem on the streets of London if it did not exist. However, it produces a fund-raising brochure which carries the heading: 'People aren't born in the gutter, they're pushed'. That is not always so. The man who is living on the street because he has walked out on a difficult family situation, when it was his clear moral duty to stay and resolve it, has not been pushed. The teenager who leaves home because his parents tell him he must be in by midnight has not been pushed. These people jumped. The Director of the Passage writes in the 1995 Annual Report:

> The cause of much of today's poverty and exclusion is not because of the inadequacies of people, but of faulty legislation—the economy has played a major part in this situation ... For some years the economy has taken precedence over people and it would appear that competitiveness and profit are more important than the human dimension.

Whilst no one would deny that some homeless people are the victims of combinations of misfortune which would have overwhelmed almost anyone, it is surely not helpful to absolve any group of welfare claimants so completely of responsibility for their own situations with such unprovable assertions.

Professor Errant

The exponent *par excellence* of the view that the system is to blame is Bob Holman. He left his position as Professor of Social Administration at the University at Bath because his Christian faith caused him to ask himself whether 'the affluence of a professor's lifestyle was inconsistent with the Christian teaching on sharing'.[11] After ten years spent working for the Children's Society on a project outside Bath he moved with his wife to Easterhouse, a sink estate outside Glasgow which would come towards the top of anyone's scale of multiple deprivation.

Of his genuine Christian commitment there could be no doubt. Whereas all the other agents of welfare provision travel in to Easterhouse, he chooses to live amidst the squalor, the pervasive crime and the gangs. However, his unwillingness to confront the moral failings of the poor who surround him is remarkable. He wrote an article for *New Statesman and Society* in which he concentrated on his experiences with one particular family, consisting of a lone mother and seven children, which was so chronically dysfunctional that it made *Crapston Villas* look like *The Waltons*. He concluded his depressing tale of fecklessness, selfishness, violence and drug abuse by saying: 'I like them all and I believe they should have a fairer deal in an unjust and unequal Britain'.[12]

There is no discussion of the extent to which the atrocious behaviour of the family members was directly responsible for most of their problems, to say nothing of the way in which such families can reduce the quality of life for everyone in their area. There is apparently no need for people to change, all that is necessary is for society to give them 'a fairer deal'.

The irony of Bob Holman's position is that, although he is a man of deep spiritual convictions who has been prepared to accept a severe drop in his own standard of living as a result of his faith, the solutions he proposes to social problems are essentially material and make few requirements of those he wishes to help. In his book *Children and Crime*[13] he gives numerous case histories of people who appear to have so little control over their lives that they require virtually limitless assistance from statutory and voluntary bodies just to survive. Self-sufficiency is not even a distant prospect. Although Holman is well aware of the extent to which family breakdown contributes to delinquency, he seems unwilling to deal with this as an aspect of personal moral behaviour which could be changed. However, there is no such reticence about blaming politicians for setting low moral standards with their sexual and financial scandals.

Holman relies heavily on a few contentious pieces of research which claim to show a close connection between crime and such factors as poverty, unemployment and even free market economics. This gives the impression that these structural variables are the main causes of criminal activity, whilst minimising the importance of issues of personal morality like family breakdown. Holman does not refer to the work of other academics who have used longer-term data to question such a connection.[14] The effect of this is to minimise the importance of the moral character of the individual. Holman does not completely exonerate his juvenile delinquents and their hopeless parents of all responsibility—the endless rehearsal of mitigating circumstances just gives that impression—but his really fierce condemnations are for the 'system':

> ... it is socially criminal that so many people are condemned to poverty ... Poverty is a millstone which drags some—but not all—into the sea of delinquency. However, the millstone can and should be released. Society can and should combat poverty.[15]

He proposes to do this through wage subsidies, minimum income and wage legislation and massive redistribution of wealth by the government. He seriously repeats Peter Townsend's proposal to remove 20 per cent of the disposable income of the wealthiest 20 per cent of the population in order to double the income of the poorest,[16] as if such a transfer could make any significant impact on the problems of the improvident, the lazy and the selfish.

Lessons from South London

In 1895 Trinity College, Cambridge opened a Mission in Camberwell, South London. Inspired by the University Settlement movement, its aim was, in the words of Montagu Butler, to bring 'the young men of a College like Trinity face to face, heart to heart, with the poorer classes of London'.[17] Toynbee Hall, the most famous of the Settlements, had opened just a few months before, but there was a big difference between the two organisations. Although it was run by a clergyman, Toynbee Hall was essentially a secular institution specialising in educational work, with no denominational or evangelical bias. The Trinity Mission, on the other hand, was intended, in the words of its first Warden, 'to meet the spiritual destitution of the metropolis',[18] and to address social problems as one aspect of evangelisation. This did not mean that the social work was taken any less seriously. As a later Warden was to explain: 'religious work that leaves out social obligations is simply a misnomer that bears no relation to life'.[19]

Lawrence Goldman concluded his official history of the Mission's first one hundred years, published in 1985, by listing some statistics of social deprivation in Camberwell today and observing:

> ... it only takes a single visit to the Parish of St George to appreciate the effects of the recent cuts in public expenditure on welfare, on education, and above all, on housing. In such circumstances there is little that the Trinity College Centre can do to ensure permanent social change for the better. That can only come when policy changes and the resources are made available to provide the jobs, the houses, the nurseries, the residential homes and the day centres that are required.[20]

The inherent hopelessness of this analysis is fairly general now in Christian welfare organisations. Had it been shared by the idealistic souls of the 1880s and 1890s who were launching the Settlement movement, it is unlikely the Trinity College Mission would have come into being in the first place.

Nothing Left To Do

We have seen how the expectations of charitable activity changed around the turn of the century. The old view that philanthropy could cope with most welfare needs, with the state filling in the gaps, was turned on its head. With 'the state as caterer-in-chief for its citizens', in C.S. Loch's contemptuous phrase,[21] the role of voluntary organisations was called into question. Should they continue to provide services in a way which would put them into direct and possibly unfavourable competition with the state? Or should they allow themselves to be sucked into the state system, becoming the junior partner in the welfare firm?

For Christian philanthropies the problem has been particularly acute. As we have seen, the emphasis on evangelical outreach and spiritual renewal may not be possible when the bills are being paid by increasingly secular statutory authorities. This has been compounded by a tendency to see problems of poverty and deprivation as the product of unjust political structures, rather than personal moral failings which can be corrected with the right advice and support. Taken to an extreme, this can result in an attempt to transfer all responsibility for social problems onto the state and away from individuals, even those who are clearly suffering as the result of personal failings which need to be addressed before any real improvement can take place.

There is then nothing left for the Christian philanthropist to do. If deprivation is no more than a material problem, there is no longer any need for the moral growth which comes from repentance and reformation of character. If social problems can only be tackled by a radical transformation of the political and economic structures, then the case for voluntary action is weak. If the government is to blame for everything, then the government will have to put it right. The concerned and caring Christian thus finds himself in a new role: that of lobbyist for increased government expenditure.

Compassion Without Tears

The politicisation of welfare has a certain obvious appeal. Helping the poor and oppressed used to mean visiting unpleasant areas and meeting people in distress. Under the new dispensation, however, these tiresome tasks can be avoided. The measure of good citizenship used to be the extent to which men and women of goodwill would give of their own time and resources to address social problems. Now, all that is required is political lobbying. A letter to your MP or local newspaper, to be followed by a trip to the Houses of Parliament, will generally suffice. Instead of putting your hand in your own pocket, you can feel virtuous by demanding higher taxes to finance increased public expenditure—which is effectively putting your hand in other people's pockets.

One of the most famous expositions of this approach, which might be described as compassion without tears, occurred in the Church of England's 1985 report *Faith in the City*.[22] It addressed itself to the same problems which had concerned philanthropists throughout the nineteenth century: the growth of an urban underclass, living in squalor, cut off from effective participation in society to the point at which they constituted a threat to social order and a challenge to the church:[23]

> We have seen areas where unemployment, poor housing and the threat of criminal violence have reached such proportions that they are like a disease: they so dominate people's thinking and feeling that no presentation of the gospel is possible which does not relate to these material deprivations.[24]

In 1890 William Booth, starting from exactly the same premise, had produced *In Darkest England*, his massive scheme for social regeneration. Just over a hundred years later *Faith in the City* addressed the same issues but came to radically different conclusions. Whereas Booth proposed a solution based on private giving coupled with spiritual renewal, the Church of England produced a list of demands for more government action:

> ... what the inner cities need more than anything else is a vote of *confidence*. It must be for the government first and foremost to demonstrate this confidence through a sustained programme of public investment.[25]

At the beginning of the report the authors pose and answer a most important question:

> The question at issue is whether the acknowledged Christian duty to 'remember the poor' should be confined to personal charity, service and evangelism directed towards individuals, or whether it can legitimately take the form of social and political action aimed at altering the circumstances which appear to cause poverty and distress. We shall argue that these are false alternatives: a Christian is committed to a form of action which embraces both.[26]

This would be an uncontroversial position, except for the fact that charity and evangelism are scarcely mentioned anywhere in *Faith in the City*. There are chapters dealing with education, employment, health and housing, each of which contains long lists of demands on national and local government, whilst making almost no mention of any contribution required from the church as an institution or from individual Christians.

Faith in the City places great emphasis on what it calls 'community'. Indeed, it is scarcely an exaggeration to say that 'community' is to *Faith in the City* what Christianity was to *In Darkest England*. However, the chapter entitled 'Social Care and Community Work' makes it clear that even 'community' work, with its traditional associations of mutual aid and the willing acceptance of responsibility, is in this analysis little more than a form of political activism:

> ... community work is not about delivering services to people ... Rather, it takes as its starting point that many of the factors combining to bring about the difficulties and injustices experienced in local communities must be located within and between the policies and practices of institutions, authorities or commercial bodies. To these corporate issues a corporate response is required.[27]

The church's involvement with community work is seen in terms of getting people to join 'tenants' associations, community councils, action groups, and ...a variety of welfare-oriented groups'.[28] It does not appear to have occurred to the authors of *Faith in the City* that there is a community outside the sphere of political action, a community in which people provide for their own needs and the needs of those less fortunate than themselves by exercising such virtues as thrift, prudence, industry and charity.[29] The church used to be keen to promote these, although the reader of *Faith in the City* will look in vain for any endorsement of a spirit of community which does not have to be subsidised by an outside body, usually the local authority.[30]

Faith in the City concluded with a list of 61 recommendations, 38 to the Church of England and 23 to the government. Those addressed to the church were vague and tended towards the construction of another tier of bureaucracy within its structure. For example, there were requests for more statistics to be collected, for a new commission on black Anglicans, for more ethnic governors on the boards of church schools and more ethnic members of the Synod and for more consultation before selling redundant churches. Above all, the report called for training: training of teachers, theological students, ministers and social workers. What all this training was supposed to achieve was not entirely clear.

However, the calls for action by government were far more specific. The report demanded an increase in the earnings disregard for supplementary benefit, an extension of the Housing Act to cover all homeless people, the funding of Law Centres as recommended by the Lord Chancellor's Committee, a Police Liaison Committee for Greater London, more public housing, an increase in the Rate Support Grant and an increase in spending on the Urban Programme generally.

The real thrust of *Faith in the City* was to influence governmental programmes and to increase public expenditure, and this was confirmed by the publication in 1995 of a ten-year follow-up entitled *Staying in the City*. This gave details of a small number of social welfare projects funded by the Church Urban Fund, which had been set up in response to *Faith in the City*, but these were almost incidental to the assessment of the impact of the report, which was principally considered in political terms. A contribution by Graham Bowpitt of Nottingham Trent University admitted that *Faith in the City*'s 'call to action' had been addressed to the nation as a whole, but that 'the bulk of the recommendations demand a policy response from the government'. This response, in Bowpitt's view, had been inadequate:

> Does this therefore mean that *Faith in the City* has failed? I believe that there are good grounds for answering 'no'. The first criterion by which the report's impact is to be judged is whether the Church has acted as an effective political opposition on urban affairs. Although it is hard to point to specific changes of policy arising from *Faith in the City*, the Government now feels obliged to take a religious perspective seriously in its policy deliberations.[31]

The notion that *Faith in the City* is to be judged by the extent to which it has affected action by government, rather than action by Christians, is confirmed by other contributors to *Staying in the City*. The Churches National Housing Coalition, formed in 1991, reported on its activities to date. These included a national lobby of parliament, publication of a handbook, the organisation of Homelessness Sunday and a response to the government's Homelessness Review in 1994. The Committee appears to have done nothing to provide housing for homeless people beyond the rather vague claim to have helped to establish over 30 'rent/guarantee schemes to rehouse homeless people in the private rented sector', and even this only amounted to publishing a handbook and organising training sessions.

The Coalition 'believes that major housing policy changes are needed ... in the area of the supply of accommodation for rent at affordable prices'.[32] Given that the Church of England is the largest landowner in the country after the Crown, there must be more effective means available to the Coalition of providing good quality housing at affordable rents than by publishing handbooks and lobbying MPs.

Poverty Consultants

The Churches National Housing Coalition was set up largely at the instigation of Church Action on Poverty (CAP), an even more vigorous campaigner for government solutions to welfare problems. In *Staying in the City*, CAP reports on its 'key achievements' as follows: organising 'six national poverty consultations', opening a parliamentary office, running Unemployment Sunday and 'a wide variety of other activities including: regular national conferences and training events, meetings with Government ministers, evidence given to Parliamentary Select Committees and the Social Security Advisory Committee, regular press briefings on poverty trends and their impact on society'.[33]

It may seem ungenerous to point out that none of these activities would involve working with poor people to help them to find a way out of their poverty. Most would not even necessitate contact with any poor people, beyond the lucky few who are chosen to appear at Church of England press conferences. It would seem that the modern Christian can express the most profound sense of solidarity with the poor without having to meet anyone below the level of a rural dean.

No Faith in the Future

The contrast between the modern approach, dragooning government into the role of big benefactor, and that which lay behind William Booth's Darkest England scheme, could hardly be greater. The Salvation Army, under Booth, was doing the work: building and running hostels, feeding the hungry, running training centres, workshops and a model farm, as well as homes for unmarried mothers, rehabilitation programmes for alcoholics and other activities. The Salvationists did not spend their time lobbying for the state to take on the work, and Booth had reservations about how good a job the state would make of it anyway (see p. 40). On the contrary, they set a standard which no state-run programme could have matched: it is significant that in 1894 the Poor Law guardians of Camberwell started sending their most hopeless cases to Booth's model farm, knowing that he might make something of them where the workhouse had failed.[34]

However, the big difference between Booth, who can be said to represent nineteenth-century evangelical Christian philanthropy, and the modern approach of compassion without tears, is not financial. Booth had to persuade well-wishers to fund all of his work, which meant that he had to be able to produce results to please the donors, but he himself would have said that the money was the least important part of the equation. The real dynamic for evangelical philanthropy came from faith, the sort of faith which believed that Christianity could change people for the better. Booth insisted, on page after page, that any attempt to deal with material deprivation which did not invoke the spiritual dimension was doomed.[35] It is this element which has disappeared from much church welfare work.

It would be untrue to say that *Faith in the City* does not mention God: six out of fourteen chapters deal specifically with church issues. However, the interest in the religious dimension of the inner city is almost exclusively historical and administrative. There is a good deal about maintenance of properties, expanding the church bureaucracy and the need to share church premises with other faiths, but nothing about the need to preach the word of God and win converts. On the contrary, the report asks:

> How far is it right to teach the Christian faith as *the* religion to be desired and believed? ... There is a possible clash between the aims of Church schools and the need for racial harmony and justice.[36]

There is a detailed discussion about the allocation of clergy within inner city parishes but, in spite of finding that the average congregation amounts to only 90 adults,[37] there is nothing about the need to increase the numbers of worshippers. In this vision of the church, the man or woman in the pew counts for little—beyond providing another potential 'community' worker.

Towards the end of the first part of *Faith in the City*, which deals with the church's role, the reader comes upon the following admission:

> ... society ... cannot be purged of its imperfections by careful planning, maintenance and repair (necessary though these are) but requires redemption through suffering and self-giving undertaken in solidarity with Christ ... the gospel, when faithfully proclaimed in word and deed, effects a transformation of individual lives, of families and of communities.[38]

This statement makes a striking impression on the reader because it does not relate to the rest of the book. In fact, it reads as if it had been mistakenly imported by 'computer error' from another book. There is no sense in which *Faith in the City* could be described as a missionary document. It does not deal with the transforming effect of religious belief upon individuals as a means of addressing social problems. The notion that unchurched inner-city dwellers are in need of salvation is not mentioned, and indeed would seem ridiculous in this context. The role of the church in addressing social problems has been reduced to that of political agitator. Not only is the connection between spiritual renewal and social progress missing, but the church does not even intend to allocate much of her own considerable financial resources. For this reason the analysis of social problems is patchy and unlikely to lead to any real improvements. *Faith in the City* should really have been called *Faith in the Government*, but, as experience has shown, that is a faith which is grounded in quicksand.

The Reversal of the Great Reversal

In Chapter 5 we looked at what has come to be known as the Great Reversal: the withdrawal from social activism by large numbers of evangelicals at the beginning of the twentieth century (see p. 64). The 1970s witnessed what can only be described as the reversal of the Great Reversal, as evangelicals re-entered the field of social reform in a process which was described by John Stott as 'the recovery of our temporarily mislaid social conscience' after 'the half century of neglect'.[39]

However, as Rachel Tingle has argued,[40] the social action of the current era is very different from that of Shaftesbury and Wilberforce, who are cited as historical precedents. The great outpouring of evangelical philanthropy and social reform which characterised the nineteenth century had been preceded by several decades of intense evangelisation, notably the preaching of John Wesley and the spread of what became known as Methodism in the second half of the eighteenth century. The impact of the Wesleyan revival on the life of the nation was immense. Alcoholism and prostitution decreased, literacy and living standards increased, as a result of widespread religious conversions.[41] The historian Taine believed that Methodism had saved England from revolution. It was from this spiritual basis that the social work grew.

However the re-entry into the field of social reform in the 1970s was not preceded or accompanied by any such movement. Far from converting large swathes of the population to strict biblical practice, the churches were themselves going through a period of uncertainty in matters of faith and morals, which seems to have become more intense with the passage of the years. When bishops doubt the resurrection and the Church of England's Board for Social Responsiblity defends 'living in sin',[42] it is doubtful if attempts by the church to re-make the structures of society will follow a biblical model. On the contrary, in such a situation political activism can easily become a convenient means of escaping from perplexing doctrinal disputes. When the churches are unable to speak with a clear voice in matters of faith and morals, criticising the government for failing in *its* supposed duties becomes a welcome distraction.

This taste for making political pronouncements *ex cathedra* has led some churchmen into the faintly ridiculous position of demanding the radical transformation of society, just at the time when the real influence of the churches is in decline. This approach is known as Kingdom thinking, which holds that the church can in some way usher in the Kingdom of God on earth through socio-political action. Given the obviously imperfect state of all human institutions, this would clearly entail a massive re-ordering of society. According to John Gladwin (now Bishop of Guildford):

> Kingdom thinking is about more than simply following the example of Jesus in His acts of mercy for the needy ... it is concerned with the structures of society, their inability to reform themselves and the need, therefore, for confrontation with them and for radical change of them ... it is concerned with the radical *transformation* of social order.[43]

Before being appointed Bishop of Guildford John Gladwin was secretary of the Church of England's Board of Social Responsibility and, as such, was

closely involved in the production of *Faith in the City*. His pre-occupation
with Kingdom thinking is reflected in that report's emphasis on structural
change to be brought about by political activism.

Concurrent with this feeling that political change will usher in the
Kingdom of God on earth is the view that charitable activity, as traditionally understood, is of little value and may even be helping to prop up an
oppressive order. According to Rev Colin Marchant of the Evangelical
Coalition for Christian Mission:

> We cannot ... engage in a paternalistic form of charity for even the best of
> charity leaves unjust social structures undisturbed, distances itself from the
> recipients and reinforces the low self-esteem of those who receive.[44]

Retraining the Good Samaritan

Faith in the City represents two important trends in Christian thinking
which impact on philanthropic work. The first is the view that the
government is the principal agent for delivering welfare services. The
second is that the main role of the church in this area is to agitate for
political action rather than to seek conversions.

Although *Faith in the City* was published in 1985 its influence is by no
means extinct.[45] It spawned a pile of related publications[46] and still has its
own office in the General Synod. The trends which it exemplified are not
confined to the established church, nor to the evangelical wing of
Christianity. They are to be found throughout the church welfare sector in
varying degrees of intensity. That is not to say that church charities are no
longer attempting to raise money from the public for their own programmes, nor that they have lost their interest in spiritual matters, but
there has been a change in emphasis in recent years.

The Bishop of Oxford takes the view that 'Taxes are a good thing and
paying them is a spiritual matter'[47] and a letter to *The Times* signed by the
Bishops of Croydon, Barking and Woolwich ressurected the old statistic of
30 per cent living in poverty and asked readers:

> ... to join us as the voice of the voiceless by insisting at our every encounter
> with politicians at all levels that they give us their personal answer to the
> question: 'what will *you* do about the forgotten 30 per cent?'[48]

One might think that the obvious answer which politicians could give to
their lordships would be: 'and what will *you* do, given the huge resources
available to the church?' It is difficult to find any scriptural justification for
the use of the machinery of the state to carry out good works. On the
contrary, the Christian conscience finds charitable expression through
personal, sacrificial giving (Matt. 5:15; James 2:15-17). The Good
Samaritan did not direct the man fallen among thieves to the nearest
official of the Roman Empire. He did not lobby for enhanced security on
the road from Jerusalem to Jericho. He gave of his own time and resources
to assist a stranger in need. Although he is often cited by churchmen in
support of demands for government spending, the Good Samaritan

provides no such precedent. As Anthony Flew has pointed out with reference to *Faith in the City*:

> The true model for the enforced transfers supported by the Commission is the legendary robber Robin Hood, who stole from the rich and—no doubt after subtracting some susbstantial handling charge—gave to the poor.[49]

The Good Samaritan is, in fact, not at all helpful to Bishops who want higher taxes, because the moral which Christ himself drew from the story was one of personal involvement, not political action. He said to the lawyer: 'Go and do likewise' (Lk. 10:37).

The De-moralisation of Society

It is particularly disappointing that the churches should be trying to off-load responsibility for social welfare onto the government now, at the very time when it is becoming increasingly obvious that the debate surrounding the failure of the welfare state is, in its most important aspects, a moral one.

Most people are familiar with the arguments about welfare dependency, which are fairly easy to grasp. The welfare system encourages and rewards the very types of behaviour which are damaging to society—dishonesty, idleness, irresponsiblity in personal relationships—while discouraging and penalising the sort of behaviour which builds up the community, such as as industry, thrift and self-restraint.

However, as David Green has argued, the demoralising effects of state welfare are not confined to the recipients: they affect the whole of society, including those who are not claimants. Prior to the advent of the wefare state it was taken for granted that people who had a reasonable income and education would allocate time and resources to their chosen charities. For many this was not a question of putting a few shillings in a collecting tin once a year but of giving a day or more each week, and perhaps even tithing the household income (see p. 15). It was in this way that the voluntary sector functioned as both a training ground for good citizenship and a nursery of the virtues. People learned to be altruistic, sympathetic and responsible. At a societal level there was a growth in the sense of community, bringing together rich and poor as members of one nation instead of two tribes. At a personal level the individual experienced the sort of moral growth which the churches used to be keen on.

For most people now questions of social welfare belong within the state sector. They take the view, not surprisingly, that, when they are being heavily taxed to pay for a state welfare Leviathan, they are not going to pay twice. Society is thus impoverished, as good citizenship is discouraged by a system funded by taxation. Taxation, being compulsory, has no moral dimension and offers no opportunities for growth. We all lose.[50]

There is No Alternative

TOWARDS the end of his life William Booth became involved with some Home Office-sponsored attempts to reclaim prisoners from their wicked ways, but he was not impressed by the approach:

> No one seems to grasp the necessity for Religion, anyway for a Religion of Regeneration. They think that with greater kindness some improvement will be effected. I think that [by] greater kindness, without some definite effort at conversion, more evil will be done than good.[1]

The repeated failure of attempts to reform criminals by showing kindness, as expressed, for example, by African safaris for juvenile delinquents, without requiring any sort of change of heart, suggests Booth was right. Unfortunately the Religion of Regeneration is conspicuous by its absence from the majority of welfare programmes today, including those which are run by religious charities.

Suffer the Little Children

In the case of the children's charities, for example, it has ceased to be an issue that the children in their care should be brought up as members of any denomination, or even as Christians at all. Such a policy would now be regarded with suspicion, as an attempt to do surreptitious evangelising. There are some who regard the early evangelical approach of their organisation with some distaste, considering that the poor were being offered bribes to be religious.

In 1943 the principal of the National Children's Home (now NCH Action for Children) could write:

> ... the Children's Home is a church in the sense that it seeks to direct the feet of those setting out on life's journey into ways of Christian discipleship.[2]

It is unlikely that NCH Action for Children would publish such a statement now. The 1994/5 Annual Report contains no reference to any such evangelical aims: in fact it scarcely mentions religion at all. The organisation is described as having 'its roots deep in the Methodist tradition, and we adhere strictly to the principles of equal opportunities' (as if these two things were synonymous), but there is no mention of any spiritual dimension to the work. NCH Action for Children reports to the Methodist Conference, which appoints its Council. The Chief Executive Officer must be a practising Christian and the Pastoral Director a Methodist Minister. However, the religious basis is not made explicit in dealing with the children in its care, but is seen rather as being implied in the quality of that care.

The changing approach of the Church of England Children's Society (now the Children's Society) is even more significant, in view of its close connection with the established church. Its 1972 Annual Report could state that:

The Christian way of life is fundamental to the Society's work. The Founder ... felt it essential that they [the children] should have faith if they were to have hope, and today the Society considers this vitally important to its daily work.[3]

The Society's Annual Reports used to carry the announcement that:

The Children's Society believes that family upbringing in the Christian faith is important to the welfare of every child, and puts this principle into practice.

However, after 1976 this statement was dropped, together with the policy of attempting to ensure a Christian upbringing for the children in the care of the Society. This is because the emphasis is now on keeping children in their own homes wherever possible, so that it becomes difficult to give any sort of religious instruction when this might conflict with what the parents believe and wish to have their children taught.

'Christianity in Action'

This is not to say that the Children's Society is no longer a Christian organisation. On the contrary, it publishes a values statement which declares that 'Our values are grounded in the words and actions of Jesus in the Gospels, especially his concern for each child'. Members of the Management Team must be practising Anglicans, there is a Chaplain who must be a priest of the Church of England, and religious services are organised for staff. However, in terms of the impact of this religious commitment on the children in its care, it is more difficult to be precise. The Society describes its work as 'Christianity in action' and 'the practical application of Christianity', but the religious dimension is implicit rather than explicit. The children would not necessarily be aware of any specifically Christian element in the work.

This reluctance to be overtly religious in approach raises questions about the advisability of the churches becoming involved in social welfare projects at all. William Booth's justification for Christian welfare work was that no one would be saved with a toothache or cold feet. The churches had to address themselves to these questions if they wanted people to be in a condition in which it was even possible for them to contemplate spiritual questions. But if the state provides a free dental service and a guaranteed income for all irrespective of employment, why should the churches get into this area at all? The spiritual dimension, which state welfare can never address, provides the only rationale for church involvement.

Contracting Out

To a certain extent, the reduced emphasis on spiritual renewal can be blamed on the contract culture of welfare. When the state or the local authority is picking up the bills, the opportunities for evangelical outreach are limited. However, we should not over-emphasise this factor, as fashions in social services come and go, and there is a great variety of approaches between different local authorities and statutory bodies. The Salvation Army's spiritual emphasis has antagonised some local authorities in the past and led to confrontational situations. In one major city during the 1970s the local authority's grudging financial support was made conditional on the Army accepting no direct applications from homeless people at one particular hostel: all referrals had to come from the authority's Housing Department. This meant that no one could be received out of office hours—a reversal of the Army's long-standing practice of immediate assistance for the needy. Furthermore, the local authority sometimes referred only very small numbers of the homeless to the Army, so the hostel was operating half empty.

However, the dominance of the hard left in local government, with its hostility towards charity in general and church charities in particular, has long since passed its peak, and the Army now finds a positive welcome for its spiritual or holistic approach. It is certainly not against any rules or laws to combine evangelism with welfare work. The fact is that, with the exception of the Salvation Army, it is scarcely ever done.

One explanation of what we might call the secularisation of religious charity is that charities must reflect the assumptions of the societies within which they operate. Charities have therefore become more secular because society has become more secular. As people have become more embarrassed to speak of spiritual matters, so the charities have muted the religious emphasis of their appeals. As the public have become less enthusiastic about charitable activity which seeks to make converts, so the evangelical dimension of the programmes has been watered down.

This cultural shift has affected more than church charities, of course; it has affected the way in which the churches themselves operate. The climate of ecumenism, coupled with an awareness of the issues raised by multi-culturalism, have made churchmen very wary of making any definite or exclusive claims for their own brand of faith. Inevitably missionary work—which was one of the largest areas of charitable fundraising in the last century—has also been affected. The idea of making converts is scarcely a part of the modern churchman's agenda, and indeed is seen as something slightly vulgar and improper. It would be unreasonable to expect charities to keep aloft the banner of the crusader when the churches which they represent have furled it up in embarrassment.

From the Dredge to the Elevator

Whatever the theological implications of this state of affairs may be, we should at least recognise that, from the strictly utilitarian consideration of welfare provision, much has been lost. The most important assumption which underlay philanthropy, and religious philanthropy in particular, in the past, was the belief that *lives could be transformed*—a point which can be appreciated even by those with no faith themselves. The Salvation Army's long-standing tradition of raising funds by selling *The War Cry* in pubs shows that even those who do not share the particular views of a denominational charity will support it if they believe it has the capacity to change lives for the better. In 1891 Commissioner Elijah Cadman, head of the Salvation Army's Social Wing, explained the work of hostels for the homeless, which he described as the 'dredge', and the 'elevators', which found work for the unemployed, in the following terms:

> By means of the dredge ... we pick the submerged up from the depths, and then we get them on the elevator, which lifts them up and up until they get on the top with a red jersey on and a flag in their hand, shouting 'Glory to God!'[4]

Even amongst philanthropists who were less overtly evangelical than the Salvationists, the view that personal reformation was the key to solving problems of welfare dependency was ubiquitous. As Samuel Smiles put in *Self-Help*:

> The highest patriotism and philanthropy consists, not so much in altering laws and modifying institutions, as in helping and stimulating men to elevate and improve themselves by their own free and independent individual action.[5]

The desire to help people by helping them to overcome their misfortunes or to reform their bad habits is one of the distinguishing characteristics of charitable assistance. The greatest disadvantage of state-run welfare systems is that they can never address problems in this way. On the contrary, state welfare cannot avoid creating perverse incentives: by offering a certain income, conditional only on the recipient entering or remaining in a state of dependency, the state stifles any tendency to self-improvement or moral reform which might exist. Instead of appealing to people's strengths, it encourages their weaknesses.

However, as charitable bodies have allowed themselves to be sucked further and further into the state sector, this distinguishing characteristic has been lost. The belief that lives can—or even should—be changed is scarcely in evidence. The charitable sector is thus unable to offer any real alternative to the welfare state, at a time when there is widespread dissatisfaction with the *status quo*.

Thomas Chalmers and the Parish Community

It was not ever thus. In 1815 Rev Thomas Chalmers, a minister of the established Church of Scotland, took up his appointment as minister of the Tron parish in Glasgow. He had spent his ministry prior to this appointment in the rural parish of Kilmany, where, as in most rural areas at that time in Scotland, life largely revolved around the parish community. In Glasgow he was shocked to find that this parish community scarcely existed any longer. Rapid industrialisation had made Glasgow the second city of the Empire, and massive population growth, mainly resulting from rural immigration, had created problems which no rural parson could have experienced. Rich and poor were separating into different parts of the city, fluctuations in the economic cycle were causing periodic mass unemployment, and, worst of all from the point of view of a devout Evangelical like Chalmers, the majority of the population were not going to church at all. There were, in fact, not enough places in all the churches in Glasgow to accommodate more than a small fraction of the population, and a combination of church-door collections, high pew-rents and the need to wear smart clothes kept the poor away. Wealthy churchgoers followed fashionable preachers, so many of those who attended a popular church would not have been members of that parish at all.

Chalmers had already become interested in the question of poor-relief before he left Kilmany, and one of the most distressing aspects of the collapse of the parish community in Glasgow, in his view, was the way in which the church had virtually abandoned its role in this area. The Scottish arrangements for poor-relief were very different from those which pertained under the English Poor Law. In England the parish was the administrative unit of the Poor Law, but the church had no involvement with its operation. In Scotland, by contrast, the church was the principal agency. The minister, together with his church elders and 'heritors', was responsible for the collection and distribution of the parish poor-relief fund, which was made up of church collections, rental of the parish 'mortcloth' for funerals and interest on bequests from pious parishioners. The authority of the parish was not absolute since its decisions were subject to review by the local sheriff courts, but for the most part decisions as to who should or should not receive assistance were being made by people who knew the applicants, and who were dispensing funds which they were responsible for raising.

In Glasgow the system was quite different. Owing to the sharp divisions of wealth within the city it was felt that poor-relief could not be managed on a parish basis. Rich parishes would have very few poor parishioners, while poor, working-class parishes would have too many. The church had therefore set up a body called the General Session which received the church-door collections from all churches and then paid out relief. However the church's efforts had been superseded by the Glasgow Town Hospital, set up in 1733 and funded through taxation, which distributed poor-relief on a much larger scale. In addition, there were many voluntary and charitable bodies which operated independently. In 1815 the church was responsible for only 7 per cent of the poor-relief distributed in Glasgow.[6]

Chalmers took the view that the large and growing numbers of paupers in Glasgow resulted from this confused and indiscriminate distribution of relief. The system was complicated and resulted in some of the more aggressive applicants getting relief from several sources, while other more deserving cases went unaided. The money was being distributed by people who were distanced from the applicants and who were administering funds they had not collected. In Chalmers' view, this was encouraging pauperism on a huge scale by undermining habits of industry, thrift and family responsibility.

Chalmers felt passionately that the answer was to restore the parish community in Glasgow. A system of poor-relief which was based on assessments by impersonal bureaucracies, and which allowed the rich to escape any contact with the poor, seemed to him a violation of the Christian ideal. In a properly functioning parish the rich would take an interest in the welfare of the poor as part of their Christian and neighbourly duty, and would offer personal, face-to-face assistance and advice in a way which would build up rather than demean. Furthermore Chalmers believed that the poor could only be truly helped to improve their condition by the sort of moral and spiritual guidance which the church was qualified, and indeed morally obliged, to give. Money, on its own, would solve nothing.

Chalmers expressed his views in a pamphlet published in 1817 and entitled *The Connexion between the Extension of the Church and the Extinction of Pauperism*. He called for the abolition of all poor-relief agencies operating outside the parish system, including the Glasgow Town Hospital and the General Session. All relief would become the responsibility of the parish, with elders visiting the poor in their homes to see who needed help, which would then be obtained, as far as possible, from private benefactors. As Stewart Brown pointed out in his biography of Chalmers, he drew an important distinction between poverty and pauperism. Poverty was an unavoidable part of the natural order—had not Christ warned that the poor would always be with us?—but:

> ... pauperism, with its legal apparatus of rights and obligations, destroyed both individual responsibility and communal benevolence ... transforming rich and poor into opposing interest groups seeking justice, not from God through his Church, but from the secular State.[7]

Chalmers article struck a chord with some influential people, including members of Glasgow's Town Council who were creating a new parish out of a section of Chalmers' Tron parish as part of a scheme to increase church accommodation in working-class areas. Chalmers was offered the ministry of the new parish of St John where he would be able to try out his theories of parish-based poor-relief in an urban setting. He accepted, on the condition that his new parish would not be obliged to send its church-door collections to the General Session. In September 1819, as soon as he had taken up his new position, Chalmers announced that there would be no further referrals from his parish to the Town Hospital for poor-relief. Those paupers who were already receiving relief from the Town Hospital would continue to draw it, but all new cases would have to be dealt with inside the parish.

Chalmers predicted a fall in the amounts of money which would have to be spent on poor-relief within the parish, as he intended to help the poor to regain self-sufficiency wherever possible, with poor-relief being kept as the last resort for those who could never support themselves, and who had no relatives who could be persuaded to accept responsibility for them. To achieve this he divided his parish into twenty-five 'proportions', with each proportion under the supervision of a deacon—a long-neglected lay office which he revived for the purpose. The deacons were to seek out and help with poor with advice, personal donations, appeals to family members to support their relatives, and assistance in finding jobs. If none of these options were available, and if the applicant was truly destitute and a legal resident of Glasgow, the deacon would consult with a second deacon and, if they decided the case was eligible, they would put it before the monthly meeting of deacons.

Pauperism in the parish began to decline. Between September 1819 and July 1823 the number of those receiving poor-relief fell from 125 to 91. The deacons were so enthusiastic about the new approach that they persuaded Chalmers, in March 1823, to take over the full expense of maintaining the parish's paupers in the Town Hospital. Going even further, in 1825 they removed the sick poor for whom they were responsible from the Hospital to care for them in the parish, using private physicians.

Chalmers achievement by this stage was extraordinary. As Brown puts it:

> For the first time in Scotland, an urban parish, in a city dependent upon a legal assessment for poor relief for over ninety years, had 'voluntarily' abolished the assessment and 'retraced' its path back to the traditional rural parish system of relief based upon church-door collections.[8]

The second prong of Chalmers attack on pauperism was education. When he had arrived in Glasgow he had been shocked to find that the parish schools, which provided an almost universal system of education for the poor in rural areas, did not exist in the city. He was determined to remedy this by using the money saved from poor-relief to start schools, as he regarded the provision of instruction, both religious and secular, as the surest long-term remedy against pauperism. Within three years he had opened four schools, providing instruction to 419 boys, or 42 per cent of the male children in the parish, in a range of academic and practical subjects. Admission was limited to children living in the parish to prevent 'outsiders' from taking advantage of the benefits which were flowing from Chalmers' renewed parish community.

Then, in January 1823, when the experiment was less than four years old, Chalmers amazed everyone by announcing that he was quitting the parish ministry altogether to take up the Chair of Moral Philosophy at St Andrew's University. His explanation was that he did not want the St John's system to become part of a personality cult, that he felt it could now survive without him, and that he could spend his time more profitably writing and arguing for its extension throughout Scotland.

The real reason appears to have been more complicated. Chalmers was a strange mixture of bull-headed determination and hyper-sensitivity to criticism. He was genuinely distressed by the continuous attacks on his St John's scheme, which became increasingly personal. He found the opposition of his fellow-clergy particularly hard to take, and came to dread meetings of the Glasgow presbytery. The last straw appears to have been the controversy which surrounded his plans to build a second church, or 'chapel of ease', in the parish in which pew-rents would be kept at a low level for the benefit of poor parishioners.

Chalmers raised the money for the chapel from private sources, but when his opponents in the Glasgow presbytery found out about it they demanded that the church-door collections for poor-relief should be seized by the municipal authorities and given to the Town Hospital, on the basis that a chapel of ease was not covered by the exemption which had been granted to St John's. Chalmers argued his case before the authorities and won his reprieve for the chapel as well as the main church, but he was deeply distressed to find his fellow-clergy still so hostile towards him.

The St John's system continued after Chalmers' departure, although it collapsed in 1837 as a result of rising debts and falling church-door collections. Chalmers blamed the ultimate failure on two things: firstly, the town council had not honoured the agreement to refund part of the taxes paid by St John's residents after the parish has taken all of its paupers out of the Town Hospital, and secondly, the magistrates had done nothing to stop paupers from other parishes moving into St Johns to take advantage of the superior arrangements.

Chalmers always regarded the St John's experiment as a huge success, and it became famous, largely through his own very popular books, as an example of welfare reform. However, his critics maintained that it had been a failure, and that poor-relief had only declined because the deacons were so hard-hearted that they would refuse to give relief even to obvious cases of distress. Chalmers replied that, in that case, it was difficult to understand why more paupers had moved into the parish than out of it throughout the period.

Because Chalmers' involvement with the project was so short, comprising less than four years, and it all took place so long ago, it will probably never be possible to establish how much good, if any, the St John's experiment achieved. However, we can be sure of one thing: Chalmers was an inspirational figure who commanded enormous respect for his work and his views throughout Britain. He was never short of supporters, who raised enormous sums for his various projects, and the founders of the Charity Organisation Society, launched in London over twenty years after his death, regarded him as a sort of patron saint.

Moral Gangrene

Chalmers regarded the poor law, particularly the English version of it, as an abomination—'a moral gangrene'[9]—which would bring out the worst in people because it was based upon a low view of human nature, assuming that no one would help his fellows unless compelled by the state to do it through taxation.[10] To Chalmers, the solution was clear. It was the business of Christians to offer a complete alternative to this system, which would be based on feelings of mutual obligation and respect, designed to help the poor out of their poverty by appealing to their strengths and by offering the sort of moral uplift which is (or should be) the stock-in-trade of the churches:

> The dearest object of my earthly existence is the elevation of the common people—humanized by Christianity and raised by the strength of their moral habits to a higher platform of human nature, and by which they may attain and enjoy the rank and consideration due to enlightened and companionable men.[11]

As we look at the role played by the churches in welfare provision today, it is this sense of 'otherness' which seems to be missing, this spiritual perspective on material needs which should separate church-based from statutory programmes of assistance. In short, the churches no longer present an alternative. They seem to be content to provide services in much the same way as the state, taking taxpayers' money and reporting to local authorities and government departments.

As levels of dissatisfaction with the performance of the welfare state rise, the search for alternative methods of welfare provision will intensify. The role of the churches, and indeed the whole voluntary sector, will become increasingly important. However, if the sector has become so compromised by its involvement with the state as to have lost its distinctive character, then it will not be able to make an effective contribution to the debate.

It is for this reason that we need to develop a fuller understanding of what voluntary action really entails, and what it signifies in a free society. An appreciation of the achievements of philanthropy is important because it gives us a historical perspective on the current problems. We need to ask, without being facetious, what people like Shaftesbury, Barnardo and Booth would have thought if they could come back today to see the organisations they founded. Of course, the world has moved on, and social conditions have changed radically, not just in the last century but in the last generation. However, the fundamental principles on which the philanthropists based their work—respect for the individual, the appeal to the best in people's characters, the encouragement to self-help and, most importantly, the conviction that people can change for the better with the right sort of encouragement—are as relevant today as ever. There are charitable bodies which are trading today on the capital which was accumulated by their founders, whilst neglecting the more important inheritance of their philosophy. If it were possible to rediscover the idealism and the convictions that motivated men and women to form those associations which provided welfare services, before the state stepped in, we might come some steps closer to solving the enormous problems which are posed by an over-stuffed and under-performing welfare state.

Notes

Introduction

1   Green, D.G., *Reinventing Civil Society: The Rediscovery of Welfare Without Politics*, Choice in Welfare Series No 17, London: IEA Health and Welfare Unit, 1993.

Chapter 1

1   Jordan, W.K., *Philanthropy in England 1480-1660: A study of the changing pattern of English social aspirations*, London: George Allen and Unwin, 1959.

2   Jordan, W.K., *Philanthropy in England: 1480-1660*, p. 55.

3   *Ibid.*, p. 114.

4   *Ibid.*, pp. 126-27.

5   *Ibid.*, pp. 139, 140 and 143.

6   For criticism of Jordan's thesis see Stone, L., *History*, XLIV, 1959, pp. 257-60; Coleman, D.C., *Economic History Review*, 2nd series XIII, 1960, pp. 113-15; Bittle, W.G. and Lane, R.T., 'Inflation and Philanthropy in England: A Re-assessment of W.K. Jordan's Data', *Economic History Review*, 2nd series XXIX, 1976, pp. 203-10.

7   Jordan, W.K., *op. cit.*, p. 119.

8   *Ibid.*, p. 114.

9   Duffy. E., *The Stripping of the Altars: Traditional Religion in England 1400-1580*, London: Yale University Press, 1992, p. 504.

10   Jones, M.G., *The Charity School Movement*, Cambridge: 1938, p. 38, quoted in Owen, D., *English Philanthropy 1660—1960*, Cambridge, Mass: Harvard University Press, 1965, p. 24.

11   Owen, D., *op. cit.*, pp. 30-31.

12   *Ibid.*, p. 45.

13   According to *Charity Trends*, published by the Charities Aid Foundation, 40 per cent of the top 500 fundraising charities are concerned with medicine and health—by far the largest group. (16th edition, 1993, Table 1). A public opinion poll on the importance of charitable activity found most support for medical research charities and least support for the arts and religious charities. (cited in Douglas, A., *British Charitable Gambling 1956-1994: Towards a National Lottery*, London: Athlone Press, 1995 p. 75.)

14 Owen, D., *op. cit.*, p. 39.

15 McClure, R.K., *Coram's Children: The London Foundling Hospital in the Eighteenth Century*, London: Yale University Press, 1981, p. 32.

16 *Ibid.*, pp. 14-15.

17 *Ibid.*, p. 35.

18 Coram was to benefit personally from the non-sectarian policy. When he had ruined himself financially by neglecting his own business to set up the Hospital, one of the Jewish governors, the financier Sampson Gideon, organised a subscription to provide him with a pension.

19 The governors fiercely denied these charges and threatened the editor with a prosecution for libel unless they were retracted. They did not know the identity of the author and the editor refused to reveal it, in spite of being threatened with a further action for criminal libel against himself. The strong reaction of the governors to the charge suggests that they were not as indifferent towards religious instruction as Johnson had implied, but nevertheless it is impossible to imagine anyone making a similar complaint concerning children in the care of Dr Barnardo a century later. For a full account see McClure, R.K., *op. cit.*, pp. 106-7 and McClure, R.K., 'Johnson's Criticism of the Foundling Hospital and its consequences', *Review of English Studies*, n.s. 27, 1976, pp. 17-26.

20 Stephen, J., *Essays in Ecclesiastical Biography*, 2 vols, London: 1849, i, p. 382, quoted in Prochaska, F., *The Voluntary Impulse: Philanthropy in Modern Britain*, London: Faber and Faber, 1988, pp. 39-40.

21 Quoted in Owen, D., *op. cit.*, p. 89.

22 *Statistics of Middle-Class Expenditure*, British Library of Political and Economic Science, Pamphlet HD6/D267 (undated: 1896?) Table IX. Quoted in Prochaska, F.K., 'Philanthropy', in Thompson, F.M.L. (ed.), *The Cambridge Social History of Britain 1750-1950*, vol. 3, Cambridge University Press, 1990, p. 358. Prochaska also cites a survey of working class and artisan families of the same decade which found that half of them were weekly subscribers to charity, and about a quarter also donated to church or chapel. (*Family Budgets: Being the Income and Expenses of Twenty-Eight British Households, 1891-1894*, 1896, p. 75.)

23 *The Times*, 9 January 1885; quoted in Owen, D., *op. cit.*, p. 469.

24 Burdett-Coutts, A.(ed.), *Women's Mission*, London: 1893, pp. 361-66, quoted in Prochaska, F., *The Voluntary Impulse, op. cit.*, p. 74.

25 Prochaska, F., 'Philanthropy', *op. cit.* pp. 384 & 358.

26 Prochaska, F., 'Philanthropy', *op. cit.*, p. 379.

27 Heasman, K., *Evangelicals in Action: An Appraisal of Their Social Work in the Victorian Era*, London: Geoffrey Bles, 1962, p. 14.

28 Owen, D., *op. cit.*, pp. 95 and 93.

29 Heasman, K., *Evangelicals in Action: An Appraisal of their Social Work in the Victorian Era*, London: Geoffrey Bles, 1962, p. 11.

30 The development of social casework has traditionally been attributed to the Charity Organisation Society and the National Society for the Prevention of Cruelty to Children, but Frank Prochaska has shown that it emerged much earlier from the work of Mrs Ellen Ranyard's Bible and Domestic Female Mission, founded in 1857. 'By 1862 there were Bible women in virtually every city in England and the idea soon spread to other parts of the world.' (Prochaska, F., 'Philanthropy' in Thompson, F.M.L. [ed.], *The Cambridge Social History of Britain: 1750-1950*, vol.3, Cambridge University Press, 1990, p. 369.)

31 Heasman, K., *op. cit.*, p. 80.

32 *Ibid*, p. 121-23.

33 Pelham, T.H.W., *Recollections of the Pre-Historic Days of the Polytechnic*, 1914, p. 19, quoted in Heasman, K., *op. cit.*, p. 123.

34 Letter from Chalmers to James Brown, 30 January 1819, quoted in Brown, S.J., *Thomas Chalmers and the Godly Commonwealth in Scotland*, Oxford: Oxford University Press, 1982, p. 138.

Chapter 2

1 For the sake of convenience, we will speak of Shaftesbury throughout this section, although he was Lord Ashley prior to 1851.

2 Quoted in Battiscombe, G., *Shaftesbury: a biography of the Seventh Earl 1801-1885*, London: Constable, 1988, p. 323.

3 Quoted in Pollock, J., *Wilberforce*, London: Constable, 1977, p. 143.

4 Quoted in Best, G.F.A., *Shaftesbury*, London: Batsford, 1964, p. 125.

5 Best, G.F.A., *op. cit.*, p. 123.

6 Battiscombe, G., *op. cit.*, p. 233.

7 Shaftesbury, Earl of, *Speeches of the Earl of Shaftesbury, K.G.*, London: Chapman and Hall, 1868, p. 279, quoted in Battiscombe, G., *op. cit.*, p. 220.

8 Castle Howard papers, 9 September 1948, quoted in Pollock, J., *Shaftesbury: The Poor Man's Earl*, London: Hodder and Stoughton, 1985, p. 90.

9   Shaftesbury was not alone in taking a spiritual view of public health
     issues. Charles Kingsley, author of *The Water Babies* and one of the
     founders of Christian Socialism, regarded the 'great and blessed plans for
     what is called sanitary reform' as a sign that 'Christ is revealing to us the
     gifts of healing far more bountifully and mercifully than even He did to the
     first apostles'. (See Kingsley, C., *Sermons on National Subjects*, 1852, p.
     35, quoted in Norman, E.R., *The Victorian Christian Socialists*,
     Cambridge: CUP, 1987, p. 57.) Such a view was not uncontroversial. 'The
     assertion that ethics and sanitation are co-ordinates was indeed a startling
     novelty, and later on the Christian Socialists were on that account accused
     of substituting a gospel of drains for the gospel of salvation.' (Gray, B.K.,
     Philanthropy and the State, London: P.S. King and Son, 1908, p. 19.)

10 Letter from Lord Shaftesbury to Rev G.H. Staite, dated 11 July 1881, a
     transcript of which survives in the NSPCC archives, reference 246/30/1.

11 Diary entry, 31 May 1856, quoted in Battiscombe, G., *op. cit.*, p. 197.

12 The 31 regional committees amalgamated to become the *National* Society
     for the Prevention of Cruelty to Children in 1889.

13 See Himmelfarb, G., *The De-moralization of Society: From Victorian
     Virtues to Modern Values*, London: IEA Health and Welfare Unit, 1995, p.
     41 and *passim*. Himmelfarb quotes the Criminal Registrar who was able to
     report in 1901: 'We have witnessed a great change in manners: the
     substitution of words without blows for blows without words; an
     approximation in the manners of the different classes; and a decline in the
     spirit of lawlessness'.

14 Shaftesbury slept under a quilt made by pupils of the ragged schools.

15 Quoted in Battiscombe, G., *op. cit.*, p. 196.

16 Quoted in Battiscombe, G., *op. cit.*, p. 302.

17 *Ibid.*

18 Letter dated 5 August 1870, quoted in Pollock, J., *Shaftesbury: The Poor
     Man's Earl*, *op. cit.*, p. 154.

19 For an exposition of the view that the restoration of religious and moral
     education in schools would require the transfer of responsibility for
     education from the state to churches and voluntary bodies see: Davies, J.,
     'Re-sacralising Education and Re-criminalising Childhood: An Agenda for
     the Year 2132' in Whelan, R.(ed.), *Teaching Right and Wrong: Have the
     Churches Failed?*, London: IEA Health and Welfare Unit, 1994. Davies
     cites a membership survey by the National Association of Head Teachers
     in 1994 which showed that seventy per cent of heads were not holding the
     daily act of worship required by law and that thirty per cent were not
     delivering the required R.E. curriculum. Fifty per cent of heads of *church*
     schools found the requirement for a daily act of worship and an R.E.
     curriculum which was broadly Christian unacceptable.

20 Pollock, J., *op. cit.*, p. 152.

21 Speech reported in *The Christian*, 28 March and 4 April 1872. Quoted in Wagner, G., *Barnardo*, London: Weidenfeld and Nicholson, 1979, p. 49.

22 Barnardo and his wife, who was responsible for the contents of the first posthumous biography, muddied the waters so effectively in everything relating to his early career that Barnardos celebrated its centenary in 1966—the wrong year.

23 Quoted in Rose, J., *For the Sake of the Children: Inside Dr Barnardo's, 120 Years of Caring for Children*, London: Hodder and Stoughton, 1987, p. 126.

24 Barnardo's refusal to turn away handicapped children on grounds of expense did not survive his death. The committee, worried by the state of indebtedness in which Barnardo had left the organisation, began to look for means of cutting back on expenses, and were able to enlist the fashionable arguments concerning supposed 'racial degeneration' to avoid the expense of caring for handicapped children. The January 1906 edition of the house magazine *Night and Day* carried an article on 'The question of alleged degeneration or race deterioration' which questioned the policy of accepting responsibility for handicapped children. In 1912 Barnardo's Homes officially excluded mentally handicapped children. (See Rose, J., *op. cit.*, pp. 135-37.)

25 Speech reprinted in Barnardo's magazine *Night and Day*, November 1987, and quoted in Wagner, G., *op. cit.*, p. 307, and in Rose, J., *For the Sake of the Children: Inside Dr Barnardo's, 120 Years of Caring for Children*, London: Hodder and Stoughton, 1987, p. 119.

26 Barnardo, T.J., *Something Attempted—Something Done*, quoted in Rose, J., *op. cit.*, p. 274.

27 Quoted in Rose, J., *op. cit.*, p. 276.

28 Quoted in Rose, J., *op. cit.*, p. 275.

29 Annual Report 1895, quoted in Rose, J., *op. cit.*, p. 278.

30 Wagner, G., *op. cit.*, p. 300.

31 Wagner, G., *op. cit.*, p. 223.

32 Wagner, G., *op. cit.*, p. 232.

33 Wagner, G., *op. cit.*, p. 236.

34 The story is related by Richard Collier in *The General Next to God: The Story of William Booth and the Salvation Army*, London: Collins, 1965, p. 50, who took it from N.G. Wymer's biography of Barnardo, *Father of Nobody's Children*, 1954, p. 27. A possible source for Wymer was an article which appeared in *The War Cry* (26 December 1925) p.5 entitled 'The

Founder and Dr Barnardo: Commencing his Efforts for the People with the Christian Mission, Dr Barnardo Found his Life's Work'. This was described as a 'continuation of Reminiscences by the late Envoy J. Fells', and locates the famous meeting of Barnardo with Jim Jarvis at the end of one of Booth's Christian Mission meetings. However, the ultimate source for the story appears to have been an anonymous letter which appeared in *The East London Observer* (28 August 1875) which attacked both Barnardo and Booth for operating without committees and implied that they were both 'making it pay' for themselves. The writer regretted that it should be necessary for private charities to do the sort of missionary work which the churches ought to have undertaken, but observed that Protestants 'prefer to leave the young to Dr Barnardo, just as they leave the adults to Mr. Booth'.

35 Booth had been known as General Booth even before the adoption of the military name and the use of military ranks, because his official title had been General Superintendent of the Christian Mission. He showed no displeasure when the contraction of this title to 'General' appeared to confer on him the authority of military command.

36 Battiscombe, G., *op. cit.*, p. 325.

37 Collier, R., *The General Next to God: The Story of William Booth and the Salvation Army*, London: Collins, 1965, p. 197.

38 *Ibid*, p. 61.

39 Quoted in Fairbank, J., *Booth's Boots: Social Service Beginnings in the Salvation Army*, London: The Salvation Army, 1983, p. 5.

40 Collier, R., *op. cit.*, p. 89.

41 Quoted in Sandall, R., *The History of the Salvation Army: Vol. III, 1883-1953, Social Reform and Welfare Work*, London: Thomas Nelson, 1955, p. 87.

42 Retrospective article by William Booth on 'nearly forty-four years' of Christian experience, published in the *All The World*, January 1889; quoted in Sandall, R., *op. cit.*, p. 65.

43 Quoted in Collier, R., *op. cit.*, p. 58.

44 Fairbank, J., *Booth's Boots: Social Service Beginnings in The Salvation Army*, London: The Salvation Army, 1983, p. 11.

45 *The Deliverer*, August 1891, p. 30, quoted in Fairbank, J., *op. cit.*, p. 25.

46 Booth, B., *Echoes and Memories*, London: Hodder and Stoughton, 1925, p. 1, quoted in Fairbank, J., *op. cit.*, p. 6.

47 Quoted in *The War Cry*, 14 September 1889 and 28 September 1889, and in Fairbank, J., *op. cit.*, p. 8.

48 *The War Cry*, 7 September 1889, p. 2, cited in Fairbank, J., *op. cit.*, pp. 8-9.

49 Booth, W., *In Darkest England and the Way Out*, London: Salvation Army, 1890, p. 107.

50 *All The World*, May 1897, p. 216, quoted in Fairbank, J., *op. cit.*, p. 39.

51 *The War Cry*, 25 September 1897, p. 3, quoted in Fairbank, J., *op. cit.*, p. 69.

52 Booth, W., *In Darkest England and the Way Out*, The Salvation Army: London, 1890, p. 17.

53 *A Brief Review of the First Year's Work*, London: The Salvation Army, 1891, p. 42, quoted in Fairbank, J., *op. cit.*, p. 113.

54 Fairbank, J., *op. cit.*, p. 115.

55 Booth, W., *op. cit.*, p. 36.

56 *The Liverpool Daily Post*, quoted in *The War Cry*, 11 October 1890, p. 7.

57 Booth, W., *op. cit.*, p. 205.

58 Loch, C.S., *An Examination of General Booth's Social Scheme*, Swan, Sonnenschein and Co, 1890.

59 Fairbank, J., *op. cit.*, p. viii.

60 Booth, W., *op. cit.*, p. 267.

61 *Ibid.*, pp. 45 and 44.

62 *Ibid.*, preface.

63 *Ibid.*, p. 80.

64 All statistics concerning the Salvation Army's social work show a tendency towards gigantism. The 1891 review of the first year of the Darkest England scheme cited 208,019 beds and meals supplied at four shelters for the most destitute dossers and 50,000 beds supplied in the shelters in Southwark and Drury Lane for those who were just slightly better off (Sandall, R., *op. cit.*, p. 105); in 1908 the annual total for beds supplied in the shelters passed two million. In 1917 over six million meals were served in cheap food depots (Fairbank, J., *op. cit.*, pp. 96 and 9).

65 Quoted in Ervine, St John, *God's Soldier: General William Booth*, London: William Heinemann, 1934, p. 784.

66 *Ibid.*

67 There is a note of desperation in the statement contained in Robert Sandall's history of the Army's social work that: 'The Salvation Army did not begin as, nor has it at any time, anywhere, become, a social reform organisation'. (Sandall, R., *op. cit.*, p. 74.)

Chapter 3

1 Speech reported in *The Christian*, 20 February 1873, and quoted in Wagner, G., *Barnardo*, London: Weidenfeld and Nicolson, 1979, p. 61.

2 Quoted in Davey, C., *A Man for All Children: The Story of Thomas Bowman Stephenson, BA, LLD, DD*, Epworth Press, 1968, reprinted NCH, 1989.

3 Quoted in Philpot, T., *Action for Children*, Oxford: Lion Publishing, 1994, p. 23.

4 Quoted in Philpot, T., *op. cit.*, pp. 23-24.

5 *The First Forty Years: A Chronicle of the Church of England Waifs and Strays Society 1881-1920*, London: SPCK, 1922, p. 2. This book is assumed to have been written by Rudolf, although it appeared anonymously, as it contains material which only he would have known about. The British Library catalogue ascribes the work to him.

6 The Society adopted 'The Children's Society' as an informal alternative title for common usage (as opposed to the Church of England Children's Society) at a meeting of the Executive Committee on 19 January 1982. As the Society operates in Wales, in conjunction with the Church in Wales, it was felt that to have 'Church of England' in the title was unacceptable. The Society's present logo and title strapline were adopted in 1987 and registered as a service mark by the Patents Office in 1993. The Society is still legally registered as the Church of England Children's Society with the Charity Commissioners, but on all printed material the name of the The Children's Society is followed by the words 'A Voluntary Society of the Church of England and the Church in Wales'.

7 *Night and Day* (Barnardo's magazine), vol. VI, p. 28, cited in Wagner, G., *op. cit.*, p. 214.

8 *Night and Day*, vol.VIII, April 1895; 'Our Waifs and Strays', June 1895, cited in Wagner, G., *op. cit.*, p. 215. The correspondence between Rudolf and Barnardo was published in Code, G., *Waifs and Strays: An Old Fable in a New Setting*, 1901.

9 *The First Forty Years, op. cit.*, Appendix 1, p. 214.

10 For much of the information in this section I am indebted to *That They May Have Life: a Brief History of the Catholic Children's Society in the Dioceses of Arundel and Brighton, Portsmouth and Southwark* , published by the Society in 1995. It is based on a longer work by Fr Edgar Dunn, who was chaplain to the Society between 1985 and 1990.

11 Bennett, J., *Father Nugent of Liverpool*, Liverpool Catholic Children's Protection Society, 1949, republished by Catholic Social Services (Archdiocese of Liverpool) 1993, p. 30.

12 *Ibid.*, p. 45.

13 Cardinal Wiseman, *Appeal to the English People*, 1850, quoted in *That They May Have Life*, *op. cit.*, p. 5.

14 Quoted in Philpot, T., *op. cit.*, p. 25.

15 Stephenson was writing in *The Wesleyan Methodist Magazine*, 1905, p. 106, quoted in Wagner, G., *op. cit.*, p. 305.

Chapter 4

1 Speech reported in *The Times*, 5 August 1872, and quoted in Best, G.F.A., *Shaftesbury*, London: Batsford, 1964, p. 112.

2 See Battiscombe, G., *Shaftesbury: A Biography of the Seventh Earl, 1801-1885*, London: Constable, 1988, p. 198. Shaftesbury was not alone in this view. In 1865, when John Ruskin put up the money for the first houses which Octavia Hill was to manage, he insisted on a return of five per cent on the capital. This was not because he needed or cared about the money, but he believed that, if the project could be made to pay, others would be prepared to invest in working-class housing and standards would rise. See Bell, E.M., *Octavia Hill*, London: Constable, 1942, p. 76.

3 Bradley, I.C., *Enlightened Entrepreneurs*, London: Weidenfeld and Nicholson, 1987, p. 1.

4 *Ibid.*, p. 91.

5 *Ibid.*, p. 137.

6 *Ibid.*, p. 129.

7 *Ibid.*, p. 131.

8 *Ibid.*, p. 147.

9 *Ibid.*, p. 187.

10 *Ibid.*, p. 3.

11 *Ibid.*, p.136.

12 *Ibid.*, p. 149.

13 *Ibid.*, p. 150.

14 *Ibid.*, pp. 190-91.

Chapter 5

1   Owen, D., *English Philanthropy 1660-1960*, Cambridge, MA: Harvard
    University Press, 1965, p. 503.

2   *Labour Leader*, 29 September 1905, quoted in Wagner, G., *Barnardo*,
    London: Weidenfeld and Nicholson, 1979, p. 299.

3   The catastrophic consequences of the decision by Parliament to pay for
    indiscriminate admissions to the Foundling Hospital in the 1750s are
    described in McClure, R.K., *Coram's Children: The London Foundling
    Hospital in the Eighteenth Century*, London: Yale University Press, 1981,
    pp. 76-136. The history of the RNLI's brief dependence on public subsidy is
    told in Warner, O., *The Life-Boat Service*, London, 1974, p. 37 ff.

4   West, E.G., *Education and the State*, London: Institute of Economic
    Affairs, second edition 1970 (1965), pp. xxvii & 132.

5   See West. E.G., *op. cit.*, p. 137 ff. The National Society described itself as
    'constrained by a deep sense of the inconvenience which would arise from
    admitting into the National Schools an official inspection not derived from
    or connected with the Authorities of the National Church'. Quoted in Gray,
    B.K., *Philanthropy and the State, or Social Politics*, London: P.S.King,
    1908, p. 140.

6   Quoted from one of Octavia Hill's Letters to her supporters in Bell, E.M.,
    Octavia Hill, London: Contable, 1942, p. 122.

7   From 'The Dwellings of the Poor', 1883, quoted in Goodwin, M. (ed.),
    *Nineteenth Century Opinion: An Anthology of Extracts from 'The
    Nineteenth Century', 1877-1901*, Penguin Books, 1951, p. 75.

8   Smiles, S., *Self Help: With Illustrations of Conduct and Perseverance*,
    London: Institute of Economic Affairs Health and Welfare Unit, 1995
    (original publication 1859), p. 178. Smiles was quoting Samuel Drew, 'the
    philosophical shoemaker'.

9   *Ibid.*, p. 179.

10 Westcott, B.F., *Lessons from Work*, London, 1901, p. 274, quoted in
    Norman, E.R., *The Victorian Christian Socialists*, Cambridge University
    Press, 1987, p. 178.

11 Westcott, B.F., *Christian Aspects of Life*, London, 1897, p. 15, quoted in
    Norman, E.R., *op. cit.*, p. 165.

12 Quoted in Mack, E.C. and Armytage, W.H.G., *Thomas Hughes*, London,
    1952, p. 202; and in Norman, E.R., *op. cit.*, p. 95.

13 For a full account see West, E.G., *Education and the State*, London: Institute of Economic Affairs, 1965, second edition with introductory essay 1970. West reproduces a letter written in 1876 by the Rector of St Paul's, Hulme to the Manchester School Board, responding to a request that the Mulberry Street Schools, which were parochial Church of England establishments, should become Board schools. The Rector objected to the fact that parochial schools, charging between 3d and 8d per child per week, were being forced out of business by Board Schools which were charging a flat 3d. He asked: 'is it right to members of Christian Churches, which have made great sacrifices of time and money to erect schools in connection with their places of worship, to set up rival schools which, as ratepayers, they are compelled to support, in addition to their having to support their own denominational schools?'. The Rector took the view that it would be better for the schools to close rather than betray the trust of those who had built them for denominational teaching. (pp. 157-159)

14 *The Bitter Cry of Outcast London, an Enquiry into the Conditions of the Abject Poor*, October 1883, published by the London Congregational Union, p. 2. Quoted in Heasman, K., *Evangelicals in Action: An Appraisal of their Social Work in the Victorian Era*, London: Geoffrey Bles, 1962, p. 53.

15 Booth, C., *Life and Labour of the People in London*, London: 1892, vol. 1, pp. 177-78.

16 'By 1907 Marshall was protesting that Booth's statistics themselves were being carelessly read and brought into use by the same scaremongers Booth had refuted. The one thing that every German now knew about England was that one million Londoners lived in poverty.' From Dennis, N., and Halsey, A.H., *English Ethical Socialism*, Oxford: Clarendon Press, 1988, p. 68.

17 Owen, D., *op. cit.*, p. 505.

18 Quoted in Webb, B., *My Apprenticeship*, 1926, p. 248, and in Owen, D., *op. cit.*, p. 505. Beatrice Webb was one of Booth's assistants on his *Survey*, and his cousin by marriage.

19 Owen, D., *op. cit.*, p. 505.

20 Booth, C., *Pauperism, a Picture; and the Endowment of Old Age, an Argument, London, 1892*, p. 148. Quoted in Owen, D., p. 505.

21 See Heasman, K., *op. cit.*, pp. 67-6 and 243-45.

22 Quoted in Owen, D., *op. cit.*, p. 509.

23 Gray, B.K., *Philanthropy and the State or Social Politics*, London: P.S. King, 1908, Editor's Preface, p. iv.

24 *Ibid*, p. 154.

25 *Ibid.*, p. 297.

26 *Ibid.*, pp. 294-95.

27 For an account of the friendly societies and the impact of legislation upon them see Green, D., *Reinventing Civil Society: The Rediscovery of Welfare without Politics*, London: Institute of Economic Affairs Health and Welfare Unit, 1993.

28 Owen, D., *op. cit.*, p. 545.

29 Beveridge, W., *Voluntary Action*, London, 1948, p. 318, quoted in Owen D., *op. cit.*, p. 574.

30 An extreme example was the Royal Surgical Aids Society which found itself almost completely redundant in a National Health Service, but with invested funds amounting to £250,000. Under the scope of *cy-près* legislation, the trustees were permitted by the court to use the funds to establish homes for the elderly. (See Owen, D., *op. cit.*, p. 573.)

31 Macadam, E., *The New Philanthropy*, London, 1934.

32 As Milton Friedman put in, in what became known as Friedman's Law, 'Everything government does costs twice as much'.

33 *Charity Trends*, Charities Aid Foundation, 11th edition, 1988, p. 114, cited in Douglas, A., *British Charitable Gambling 1956-1994: Towards a National Lottery*, London: Athlone Press, p. 70.

34 McQuillan, J. (ed.), *Charity Trends*, Charities Aid Foundation, 16th edition, 1993, p. 51, cited Douglas. A., *Ibid.*

35 Prochaska, F., *The Voluntary Impulse: Philanthropy in Modern Britain*, London: Faber and Faber, 1988, p. 4.

36 Quoted in Prochaska, F., *Philanthropy and the Hospitals of London: The King's Fund 1897-1990*, Oxford: The Clarendon Press, 1992, p. 110.

37 *Voluntary Hospitals [Cave] Committee* (Cmnd 1335) 1921, p. 8.

38 Spielman, M.A., 'The importance of preservation of the voluntary principle in child saving and rescue work', Reformatory and Refuge Union Conference Report, 1921, quoted in Philpot, T., *Action for Children: The Story of Britain's Foremost Children's Charity*, Oxford: Lion Books, 1994, p. 64.

39 Quoted *ibid.*

40 Special meeting of the Council, 20 March 1946, quoted in Rose, J., *For the Sake of the Children: Inside Dr Barnardo's, 120 years of caring for children*, London: Hodder and Stoughton, 1987, p. 206.

41 Quoted *ibid.*, p. 202.

42 Nathan Report, Q.6850, quoted in Owen, D., *op. cit.*, p. 543.

43 Battiscombe, G., *Shaftesbury: a biography of the Seventh Earl*, London: Constable, 1974, p. 102.

44 For an account of the Great Reversal see Stott, J., *Issues Facing Christians Today*, Marshall Pickering, 1984, p. 6. Stott cites Moberg, D.O., *The Great Reversal: Evangelism versus Social Concern*, London: Scripture Union, 1972. The term was first used by the American church historian Timothy L. Smith.

Chapter 6

1   Hall, M.P. and Howes, I.V., *The Church in Social Work: A Study of Moral Welfare Work Undertaken by the Church of England*, London: Routledge & Kegan Paul, 1965, p. 1.

2   *Ibid.*, pp. 250-51.

3   *Ibid.*, p. 246.

4   *Ibid.*, pp. 54-55, quoting from 'The Unmarried Mother', *Planning*, No. 255, 13 September 1946, p. 10.

5   *Ibid.*, p. 55. The letter, dated 4 October 1946, from Miss Ena Steel, was never published.

6   Taylor-Thompson, D., *Mildmay: The Birth and Rebirth of a Unique Hospital*, London: Mildmay Mission Hospital, 1992, p. 15.

7   In the financial year 1988\89 the government spent £50.07 on health education and research into heart disease in relation to each person who died from heart disease. Spending on health education and research into AIDS in relation to each person who died from AIDS came to £289,755.87. See Whelan, R., 'The AIDS Scandal', *Economic Affairs,* Vol. 11, No. 4, London: Institute of Economic Affairs, June 1991.

8   Taylor-Thompson, D., *op. cit.*, p. 36.

9   *The Old Malvernian*, 1898. quoted in Watherston, P. , *A Different Kind of Church: The Mayflower Family Centre Story*, London: Marshall Pickering, 1994, p. 17.

10 Watherston, P., *op. cit.*, p. 23, quoting Kennedy Cox, R., *Docklands Saga*, Hodder and Stoughton, 1955, p. 66.

11 *Ibid.*, p. 106.

12 *Ibid.*, pp. 115-16.

13 *Ibid.*, p. 174.

14 *Ibid.*, pp. 197-98.

Chapter 7

1   Holloway, G., 'Chief Executive's Statement', The Shaftesbury Society's Annual Report 1994-5, p. 3.

2   Arnold Brown, Letters to the Editor, *The Times*, 27 May 1981.

3   Letter from Roger Singleton to the author, 23 May 1996.

4   Downey, R., 'Gay Foster Ban Sparks Protest Resignations', *Community Care*, 3-9 November 1994.

5   Booth, W., *In Darkest England and the Way Out*, London: Salvation Army, 1990, p. 251.

6   *The Deliverer*, February 1895, p. 124, quoted in Fairbank, J., *Booth's Boots: Social Service Beginnings in the Salvation Army*, London: The Salvation Army, 1983, p. 61.

7   Taylor-Gooby, P. , 'Welfare outside the state', *British Social Attitudes, the 11th report*, Aldershot: Dartmouth Publishing Company, 1994, p. 29. Interestingly, 52 per cent of respondents thought that the lifeboat service should be provided either entirely or mainly by the government, in spite of the fact that in the UK this is already provided on an entirely charitable basis by the Royal National Lifeboat Association.

8   'Speaking broadly and after all due deductions made, one may say that character is the key to circumstances, he therefore that would permanently mend circumstances must aim at character. All that can be done externally to remove obstacles and improve circumstances should be done, but there will be no lasting betterment without the internal change.' From the 23rd Report of the Charity Organisation Society, 1891, p. 9, cited in Gray, B.K., *Philanthropy and the State*, London: P.S. King, 1908, p. 115.

9   Smiles, S., *Self-Help*, London: Institute of Economic Affairs Health and Welfare Unit, 1996 (first edition 1859), p. 2.

10 Quoted in Bradley, I.C., *Enlightened Entrepreneurs*, London: Weidenfeld and Nicholson, 1987, p. 51.

11 Quoted in Cleave, M., 'The Good Man of Glasgow', *The Daily Telegraph*, Magazine, December 1994, pp. 20-23.

12 Holman, B., 'Family Man', *New Statesman and Society*, 8 December 1995, p. 17.

13 Holman, B., *Children and Crime*, Oxford: Lion Publishing, 1995.

14 e.g. Dennis, N. and Erdos, G., *Families Without Fatherhood*, London: Institute of Economic Affairs Health and Welfare Unit, 1992; Dennis, N., *Rising Crime and the Dismembered Family*, London: Institute of Economic Affairs Health and Welfare Unit, 1994; Hirschi, T., *Causes of Delinquency*, University of California Press, 1969; Wilson, J.Q., *Thinking About Crime*, New York: Basic Books, 1983; Wilson, J.Q., *Crime and Public Policy*, San Francisco: ICS Press, 1984.

15 *Children and Crime, op. cit.*, pp. 73 & 76.

16 *Ibid.*, p. 208.

17 Speech by Montagu Butler at a fundraising meeting for the Mission held at Devonshire House, Piccadilly, on 14 March 1893. Quoted in Goldman, L., *Trinity in Camberwell: A History of the Trinity College Mission in Camberwell 1885-1985*, Cambridge: Trinity College, p. 9.

18 From an article by Rev Norman Campbell in the magazine of St. George's parish, Camberwell, May 1886, quoted in Goldman, L., *op. cit.*, p. 8.

19 From the Warden's Report, 1921, of Rev P.M. Herbert, quoted in Goldman, L., *op. cit.*, p. 9.

20 Goldman, L., *op. cit.*, p. 46.

21 Clay, A. (ed.), *A Great Ideal and its Champion: Papers and Addresses by the Late Charles Stewart Loch*, 1923, p. 221, quoted in Woodroffe, K., *From Charity to Social Work in England and the United States*, London: Routledge and Kegan Paul, 1962, p. 39.

22 *Faith in the City: A Call for Action by Church and Nation*, The Report of the Archbishop of Canterbury's Commission on Urban Priority Areas, London: Church House Publishing, 1985.

23 The following analysis is principally concerned with the relationship of *Faith in the City* to the tradition of Christian philanthropy. For a critique of its sociological basis see Marsland, D., *Fact and Fancy in Social Analysis*, Transaction Publishers, forthcoming; for further discussion of the approach to welfare work of some contemporary Christian charities see Marsland, D., *Welfare or Welfare State?*, London: Macmillan, 1996.

24 *Faith in the City, op. cit.*, p. 51.

25 *Ibid.*, p. 175.

26 *Ibid.*, p. 48.

27 *Ibid.*, pp. 284 & 283.

28 *Ibid.*, p. 288.

29 For further discussion of the essential separateness of community and political action see Green, D.G., *Community Without Politics*, London: IEA Health and Welfare Unit, 1995.

30 'We believe that a primary responsibility lies with the borough or district councils ... to develop cross-party support for a serious commitment to community work and to resource such programmes adequately.' *Faith in the City*, op. cit., p. 288.

31 Bowpitt, G., in Jones, H. and Lansley, J. (eds.), *Social Policy in the City*, Avebury, 1995, quoted in *Staying in the City: Faith in the City ten years on*, a report by the Bishops' Advisory Group on Urban Priority Areas, London: Church House Publishing, 1995, pp. 29-30.

32 *Staying in the City*, op. cit., p. 99.

33 *Staying in the City*, op. cit., p. 101.

34 See Fairbank, J., op. cit., p. 164.

35 'I have nothing to say against those who are endeavouring to open up a way of escape without any consciousness of God's help. For them I feel only sympathy and compassion. In so far as they are endeavouring to give bread to the hungry, clothing to the naked, and above all, work to the workless, they are to that extent endeavouring to do the will of our Father which is in Heaven ... But to be orphaned of all sense of the Fatherhood of God is surely not a secret source of strength. It is in most cases—it would be in my own—the secret of paralysis.' (*In Darkest England and the Way Out*, Preface and p. 35.)

36 *Faith in the City*, op. cit., pp. 305 & 307.

37 *Faith in the City*, op. cit., p. 33.

38 *Ibid.*, p. 70.

39 Stott, J., *Issues Facing Christians Today*, Marshall, 1984, p. xi.

40 Tingle, R., 'Evangelical Social Action Today: Road to Recovery or Road to Ruin?' in Tinker, M. (ed.), *The Anglican Evangelical Crisis: A Radical Agenda for a Bible Based Church*, Edinburgh: Christian Focus, 1995, pp. 186-202.

41 See Bready, J.W., *England Before and After Wesley*, London: Hodder and Stoughton, 1939.

42 See *Something to Celebrate: Valuing Families in Church and Society*, A Report of a Working Party of the Board for Social Responsibility, London: Church House Publishing, 1995: 'The wisest and most pactical way forward therefore may be for Christians both to hold fast to the centrality of marriage and at the same time to accept that cohabitation is, for many people, a step along the way towards that fuller and more complete

commitment ... The first step the Church should take is to abandon the phrase "living in sin"' (pp. 115 & 117).

43 Gladwin, J., *Towards a New Social Revolution*, Frontier Youth Trust paper, undated, p. 5, quoted in Tingle, R., *op. cit.*, p. 200.

44 Marchant, C., *Signs in the City*, London: Hodder and Stoughton, 1985, p. 124.

45 The Anglican authorities clearly still regard the publication of the book as an epoch-making event. *Staying in the City* asks its readers: 'Can you remember where you lived, what you were doing when *Faith in the City* came out? When did you first hear about it? What did you think or feel?' (*op. cit.*, p. 37)

46 See *Staying in the City*, *op. cit.*, Bibliography, p. 136.

47 Harries, R., 'Praise be to Taxes, the Sign of a Truly Civilised Society', *The Times*, 15 October 1994.

48 'Today's Poverty, Tomorrow's Tax Cuts', *The Times*, letters, 8 November 1995,

49 Flew, A., 'State Welfare and Individual De-Moralization', *Journal des Economistes and des Etudes Humaines*, Paris, vol. 6, No. 1, March 1995, p. 179.

50 Green, D.G., *Community Without Politics: A Market Approach to Welfare Reform*, London: IEA Health and Welfare Unit, 1995.

Conclusion

1 Quoted in Ervine, St John, *General William Booth*, London: William Heinemann, 1934, p. 805.

2 Litten, J.H., *Blueprints: The Reconstruction Plans of the National Children's Home*, National Children's Home, 1943, quoted in Philpot, T., *Action for Children: The Story of Britain's Foremost Children's Charity*, Oxford: Lion Publishing, 1994, p. 83.

3 Annual Report for 1972, The Church of England Children's Society.

4 *The War Cry*, 14 March 1891, p. 7, quoted in Fairbank, J., *Booth's Boots: Social Service Beginnings in the Salvation Army*, London: The Salvation Army, 1983, p. 113.

5 Smiles, S., *Self-Help, With Illustrations of Character, Conduct and Perseverance*, London: Institute of Economic Affairs Health and Welfare Unit, 1996 (first edition 1859), p. 2.

6   Cleland, *Annals of Glasgow*, i, 270-3, cited in Brown, S.J., *Thomas Chalmers and the Godly Commonwealth in Scotland*, Oxford University Press, 1982, p. 98.

7   Brown, S.J., *op. cit.*, p. 120.

8   *Ibid.*, p. 134.

9   Chalmers, T., *The Sufficiency of a Parochial System, without a Poor Rate, for the Right Management of the Poor*, Glasgow, 1841, in *Collected Works*, xxi, p. 140, quoted in Brown, S.J., *op.cit.*, p. 294.

10 See Chalmers, T., *The Influence of Bible Societies on the Temporal Necessities of the Poor*, Edinburgh, 1814.

11 Speech reported in *The Scotsman*, 25 January 1834, quoted in Brown, S.J., *op.cit.*, p. 232.